# JESUS
### AND THE
# MESSAGE
### OF THE
# NEW TESTAMENT

# JESUS
## AND THE
# MESSAGE
## OF THE
# NEW TESTAMENT

JOACHIM JEREMIAS

*Edited by K. C. Hanson*

FORTRESS PRESS

MINNEAPOLIS

JESUS AND THE MESSAGE OF THE NEW TESTAMENT

Chapters of this book have been published by Fortress Press:
    "Searching for the Historical Jesus" (chapter 1) was originally published as *The Problem of the Historical Jesus,* Facet Books—Biblical Series 13, Fortress Press. Copyright © 1964 Fortress Press.
    "The Sermon on the Mount" (chapter 2) was originally published in North America as *The Sermon on the Mount,* Facet Books—Biblical Series 2, Fortress Press. Copyright © 1963 Fortress Press.
    "The Lord's Prayer" (chapter 3) was originally published as *The Lord's Prayer,* Facet Books—Biblical Series 8, Fortress Press. Copyright © 1964 Fortress Press.
    "The Central Message of the New Testament" (Chapter 4) was originally published as *The Central Message of the New Testament,* Charles Scribner's Sons, 1965; first Fortress Press edition, 1981. Copyright © 1965 Joachim Jeremias.

Cover art: *The Green Christ* (*Breton Calvary*), Paul Gauguin, 1889, canvas (92 x 73.5 cm.). Copyright © Erich Lessing /Art Resource, New York. Musées Royaux des Beaux-Arts, Brussels, Belgium. Used by permission of Art Resource.

Cover design: Joe Bonyata
Book design: Zan Ceeley

ISBN 0-8006-3469-1

Manufactured in the U.S.A.                                                    AF 1–3469

06    05    04    03    02    1    2    3    4    5    6    7    8    9    10

# Contents

# Acknowledgments

Chapter 1 was first published as "The Problem of the Historical Jesus" in *Expository Times* 69 (1958) 333–39, translated by Norman Perrin. Jeremias made additions and changes in subsequent German editions, and John Reumann updated the translation for *The Problem of the Historical Jesus*, Facet Books—Biblical Series 13 (Philadelphia: Fortress Press, 1964). The German edition appeared as *Das Problem des historischen Jesus*, Calwer Hefte 32 (Stuttgart: Calwer, 1960).

Chapter 2 was first published as *Die Bergpredigt*, Calwer Hefte 27 (Stuttgart: Calwer, 1959). Jeremias delivered it in English as the Ethel M. Wood Lecture at the University of London on March 7, 1961. It was first published in English as *The Sermon on the Mount*, translated by Norman Perrin (London: Athlone, 1961). The first American edition appeared as *The Sermon on the Mount*, Facet Books—Biblical Series 2 (Philadelphia: Fortress Press, 1963).

Chapter 3 began as a lecture given at Cambridge University in May 1957. It was then published as "The Lord's Prayer in Modern Research" in *Expository Times* 71 (1960) 141–46, translated by Norman Perrin. The translation was revised by John Reumann and published as *The Lord's Prayer*, Facet Books—Biblical Series 8 (Philadelphia: Fortress Press, 1964). The German edition was published as *Das Vater Unser im Lichte der neueren Forschung*, Calwer Hefte 50 (Stuttgart: Calwer, 1962).

Chapter 4 began as the Hewett Lectures of 1965 at Union Theological Seminary, New York; Episcopal Theological School, Cambridge; and Andover Newton Theological School. It was published as *The Central Message of the New Testament* (New York: Scribner, 1965; Philadelphia: Fortress Press, 1991).

Chapters 1, 2, and 3 are published with the kind permission of the Jeremias family.

# Abbreviations

## Modern

| | |
|---|---|
| *ABD* | *Anchor Bible Dictionary* |
| *ANET* | *Ancient Near Eastern Texts Relating to the Old Testament,* 3rd ed. |
| ANTC | Abingdon New Testament Commentary |
| *ATR* | *Anglican Theological Review* |
| BFCT | Beiträge zur Förderung christlicher Theologie |
| *BJRL* | *Bulletin of the John Rylands Library* |
| BZNW | Beihefte zur ZNW |
| CC | Continental Commentaries |
| FBBS | Facet Books—Biblical Series |
| FCBS | Fortress Classics in Biblical Studies |
| FOTL | Forms of the Old Testament Literature |
| HTIBS | Historic Texts and Interpreters in Biblical Scholarship |
| *HTR* | *Harvard Theological Review* |
| GBS | Guides to Biblical Scholarship |
| *IDB* | *Interpreter's Dictionary of the Bible* |
| *JBL* | *Journal of Biblical Literature* |
| *JQR* | *Jewish Quarterly Review* |
| JSNTSup | Journal of the Study of the New Testament Supplement Series |
| LCC | Library of Christian Classics |
| NRSV | New Revised Standard Version |
| NTAM | New Testament Archaeology Monograph |
| NTD | Das Neue Testament Deutsch |
| NTR | New Testament Readings |
| NTTR | New Testament Tools and Studies |
| *RGG³* | *Die Religion in Geschichte und Gegenwart,* 3rd ed. |
| RSV | Revised Standard Version |
| SBL | Society of Biblical Literature |

| SBLSBS | SBL Sources for Biblical Studies |
|---|---|
| SBLMS | SBL Monograph Series |
| SBT | Studies in Biblical Theology |
| SHT | Studies in Historical Theology |
| SNTSMS | Society for New Testament Studies Monograph Series |
| StPB | Studia Post-Biblica |
| SUNT | Studien zur Umwelt des Neuen Testaments |
| *TDNT* | *Theological Dictionary of the New Testament* |
| ThBü | Theologische Bücherei |
| *TLOT* | *Theological Lexicon of the Old Testament* |
| *TLZ* | *Theologische Literaturzeitung* |
| WUNT | Wissenschaftliche Untersuchungen zum Neuen Testament |
| *ZNW* | *Zeitschrift für die neutestamentliche Wissenschaft und die Kunde der älteren Kirche* |
| *ZTK* | *Zeitschrift für Theologie und Kirche* |

## ANCIENT

| 1QH | Hymn Scroll (*Hodayot*) 1QHymns[a] |
|---|---|
| 1QpHab | Habakkuk Commentary |
| 1QS | Community Rule (*Serek ha-Yaḥad*) |
| *Adv. haer.* | Ignatius, *Adversus haereses* (*Against Heresies*) |
| *b.* | Babylonian Talmud (*Babli*) |
| *Bar.* | *Baraita* |
| *Ber.* | *Berakot* |
| *Bib. Ant.* | Pseudo-Philo, *Biblical Antiquities* |
| *B. Qam.* | *Baba Qamma* |
| *Ep.* | Pliny, *Epistles* |
| *Jub.* | *Jubilees* |
| LXX | Septuagint |
| *m.* | Mishnah |
| *Magn.* | Ignatius, *Letter to the Magnesians* |
| par. | parallel/s |
| *Qidd.* | *Qiddušin* |
| *Ref.* | Hippolytus, *Refutatio omnium haeresium* (*Refutation of All Heresies*) |
| *Šabb.* | *Šabbat* |
| *Sanh.* | *Sanhedrin* |
| *Syr. Bar.* | *Syriac Baruch* |
| *Ta'an.* | *Ta'anith* |
| *T. Jud.* | *Testament of Judah* |
| *T. Levi* | *Testament of Levi* |

# Editor's Foreword

Few biblical scholars have had the impact on their era that Joachim Jeremias did over the course of the twentieth century. His numerous works spanned every aspect of the discipline, covering New Testament exegesis and theology, archaeology, Greek and Aramaic linguistics, textual criticism, Dead Sea Scrolls, rabbinic studies, and the history of early Christianity. Not only a major academic figure, Jeremias confronted the political and social issues of his day. During World War II, he was a member of the Confessing Church along with such figures as Karl Barth, Rudolf Bultmann, and Dietrich Bonhoeffer, the movement that refused to cooperate with the Third Reich and state control of the churches. After the war, he played a significant role in reorganizing the University of Göttingen.

Jeremias was born in Dresden, Germany, on September 20, 1900, as the new century dawned. The son of a Lutheran pastor, Dr. Friedrich Jeremias, he was also the nephew of the Semitist and ancient Near Eastern scholar, Dr. Alfred Jeremias. From the ages of ten to fifteen, Jeremias lived in Jerusalem, where his father was the pastor/dean (Propst) of the German congregation of the Erlöserkirche (Church of the Redeemer). He completed his Dr.phil. in 1922 and his Dr.theol. in 1923, both at the University of Leipzig. His mentor (*Doktorvater*) was Gustaf Dalman, the renowned scholar of ancient Palestinian culture.

He began his teaching career in 1922 at the Theological Seminary of the Brüdergemeinde in Herrnhut, near Dresden. In 1924 he became a lecturer (*Dozent*) in Riga, Latvia, at the Herder Institute. He completed his *Habilitationschrift* at Leipzig in 1925, where he was also made *Dozent*. He went to the University of Berlin as an associate professor (*ausserordentlicher Professor*) in 1928, where he was also appointed director of the Institutum Judaicum. And in 1929 he was appointed full professor at the University of Griefswald. After five years at Griefswald, he took an appointment at the University of Göttingen, where he spent the rest of his career. From 1948 he was a member of the Göttingen Academy of Sciences, and from 1956 he convened the Septuagint Commission in Göttingen.

Internationally respected by the academy, Jeremias was highly honored for his work. He was awarded the Burkitt Medal for Biblical Studies by the British Academy, and he received honorary doctorates from the universities of Leipzig, St. Andrews, Uppsala, and Oxford. Furthermore, he was made a member of the Royal Dutch Academy of Sciences and the British Academy. And in 1970 he was made an honorary fellow of the Deutsche Verein zur Erforschung Palästinas (German Society for Palestinian Research). His colleagues and students produced volumes of essays in his honor (*Festschriften*) to celebrate both his sixtieth and seventieth birthdays: *Judentum, Urchristentum, Kirche* (1960), and *Der Ruf Jesu und die Antwort der Gemeinde* (1970).

Several threads run through Jeremias's work. He attempted to reconstruct the Aramaic substratum of Jesus' sayings to reach Jesus' actual voice (*ipsissima vox*). This is evident in the chapters in this book, as well as fundamental in *The Parables of Jesus, The Eucharistic Words of Jesus,* and *The Prayers of Jesus.* He researched the Hebrew Bible, Pseudepigrapha, Apocrypha, Dead Sea Scrolls, and rabbinic works for comparisons and contrasts to the teachings of Jesus and the earliest churches, and this is especially evident in his twenty-eight articles in *The Theological Dictionary of the New Testament* (edited by Gerhard Kittel and Gerhard Friedrich). This also led him to investigate the noncanonical sayings of Jesus in *Unknown Sayings of Jesus.* Unlike many of his contemporaries (notably Bultmann), he argued strongly for the recovery of Jesus' teachings as foundational for theology.

Both the social world and archaeology of the first century intensely interested Jeremias. This was no doubt the result of having lived in Jerusalem as a boy, as well as a product of his research while a fellow of the Deutsches Evangelisches Institut für Altertumswissenschaft des Heiligen Landes (German Evangelical Institute for Research in Antiquity of the Holy Land) in 1931–32. These experiences informed one of his most enduring works, *Jerusalem in the Time of Jesus,* but also in his studies of Golgotha, the pool of Bethesda, Caesarea, and Megiddo.

An active professor as well as scholar, he mentored many students through their doctorates. His most famous student in Britain and the U.S. was Norman Perrin, who taught for many years at the University of Chicago. Among his Continental doctoral students, the names of Eduard Lohse, Bernhard Lohse, Christoph Burchard, and Elias Bickerman stand out. Although not his student, Martin Hengel was profoundly influenced by Jeremias's work as well. Jeremias's three sons also pursued careers in biblical studies: Jörg, Christian, and Gert. After his retirement in 1968, Jeremias moved to Tübingen, where he died on September 6, 1979. More than twenty years after his death, his work continues to inform and challenge us.

The reader should be aware that I have edited Jeremias's essays in a number of ways. Most importantly, I have (1) added footnotes (marked by square brackets) and bibliographies in order to bring the reader up-to-date in the discussions; (2) employed the RSV for most biblical translations; (3) added a few references that were unclear in Jeremias's text (often available from his other writings); and (4) added indexes of authors, ancient documents, and foreign terms and phrases. I have also made occasional modifications in the RSV quotations by changing RSV's "LORD" to "Yahweh" and changing words such as "thou" to "you." The reader will also note some minor overlaps between the chapters, which is due to their origin as independent essays and lectures.

I would like to express my gratitude to John Reumann and the late Norman Perrin for the work they did in translating and editing the earlier editions of these essays. And I thank Professor Jörg Jeremias of the University of Marburg for his kind cooperation and permission to reprint his father's work.

K. C. Hanson

# 1

# The Search for the Historical Jesus

To anyone unaware of the controversy, the question about whether the historical Jesus and his message have any significance for the Christian faith must sound absurd. No one in the ancient church, no one in the church of the Reformation period, and of the two succeeding centuries thought of asking such a question. How is it possible that today this question is being seriously considered and even occupies a central place in New Testament debate? In fact, in many quarters it is being answered with a decisive negative. A widely held theological position maintains that the historical Jesus and his message have no—or at least no decisive—significance for the Christian faith. I ask: (1) Why is such a point of view possible? How has it arisen? What is its basis? (2) What can be said by way of criticism about it? And (3) What is the relation between the good news of Jesus and the proclamation of the church?[1]

## The Theology of the Kerygma

In order to understand the "theology of the kerygma," as represented by Rudolf Bultmann and his school, it is necessary to retrace the route by which this position has been reached.[2] I shall attempt here to sketch that route in broad outline.

### Hermann Samuel Reimarus

The problem of the historical Jesus is of recent origin; the date of its birth can be precisely fixed at 1778—which tells us that the problem of the historical Jesus is a child of the Enlightenment. Previous centuries held fast to the position that the Gospels give us absolutely reliable information about Jesus; they saw no problem here. New Testament study of the Gospels in the two centuries before the Enlightenment essentially confined itself to the task of paraphrasing and harmonizing the four Gospels.

1

In practice, New Testament exegesis was a handmaid to the study of dog-
matics. At the end of the eighteenth century it was first recognized that the
historical Jesus and the Christ proclaimed in the Gospels and by the church
are not the same. This was announced by Hermann Samuel Reimarus, with
brutal candor. Born in Hamburg in 1694, he was a professor of Oriental languages, not a theologian. He died in 1768 in his native city. At his death he left
a manuscript that came into the hands of Gotthold Ephraim Lessing, who,
between 1774 and 1778, published seven excerpts from it. The seventh piece
was titled "Concerning the Intention of Jesus and His Disciples: Another Fragment by the Anonymous Author from Wolfenbüttel."[3]

We must, says Reimarus, distinguish between the aim of Jesus, that is, the
purpose he set for himself, and the aim of his disciples. Jesus' purpose must be
understood in the light of the cry from the cross, "My God, my God, why have
you forsaken me?"—words that proclaimed the failure of his purpose. That is
to say, Jesus was a Jewish political Messiah who sought to set up an earthly
kingdom and to deliver the Jews from a foreign yoke. His cry from the cross
shows that his "aim" had not been achieved. The "aim" of his disciples was
totally different. Confronted by the collapse of their dreams, what were they to
do? They had no wish to return to their trades. But how were they to live? They
contrived to steal the corpse of Jesus and, by inventing the message of his resurrection and return, gathered adherents. According to Reimarus, it was the
disciples, therefore, who created the figure of Christ.

Great agitation followed upon the publication of this hate-filled pamphlet,
and it rightly met with general rejection. Hate is no guide to historical truth.
Nevertheless, Reimarus, the outsider, had been the first to perceive clearly a
fact that had previously been overlooked. He had seen that the Jesus of history
and the Christ preached by the church are not the same. History and doctrine
are two different things. The problem of the historical Jesus starts with
Reimarus. Albert Schweitzer rightly titled the first edition of his history of the
study of Jesus' life "From Reimarus to Wrede."[4]

## From Reimarus to Kähler

Reimarus's portrayal of the historical Jesus was clearly absurd and amateur-
ish. Jesus was no political revolutionary. Our sources bear unambiguous and
trustworthy testimony to the fact that he was sharply opposed to the nation-
alistic Zealot tendencies in the world of his day. Still, in his contention that the
historical Jesus was different from the Christ as depicted in the Gospels
(notably in John), Reimarus had raised a question that could not be evaded,
namely: Who really was Jesus of Nazareth?

The study of the life of Jesus in which the Enlightenment now engaged
sought to answer precisely this question. This study was inspired by a liberal

theology and, indeed, represented a revolt against ecclesiastical doctrine. The whole scholarly activity, centered on the historical Jesus, represented an attempt to break loose from dogma. The battle cry was, "Back to Jesus, the man from Nazareth!" Not christological dogma, but the personality and religion of Jesus were the decisive factors.

Under the aegis of this rallying cry a multitude of lives of Jesus were written, and we smile as we read them today. These lives vary greatly. The rationalists pictured Jesus as a preacher of morality, the idealists as the ideal Human; the aesthetes extolled him as the master of words; and the socialists as the friend of the poor and as the social reformer, while the innumerable pseudo-scholars made him a fictional character.[5] Jesus was modernized. These lives of Jesus are mere products of wishful thinking. The final outcome was that every epoch and every theology found in the personality of Jesus the reflection of its own ideals, and every author the reflection of his own views. What had gone wrong? It was that, unconsciously, doctrine had been replaced by psychology and fantasy. For all these lives of Jesus have one thing in common: their delineation of the personality of Jesus had been achieved by means of psychology and fantasy. The main share of the responsibility rests not with the sources alone but with the modern writers' uncontrolled psychologizing. It was a real tragedy that Albert Schweitzer, who throughout his whole book had exposed with ruthless insight the true nature of this wishful thinking, should himself have been ensnared by the fallacy of psychological reconstruction when he interpreted Matthew 10:23 to mean that Jesus' disappointment concerning his expectations of the imminent parousia brought the great turning point in his life,[6] leading him to embark upon the way of the cross as the means to force the coming of God's kingdom.[7]

At first, the so-called positive theology wisely confined itself essentially to warding off these attempts at reconstruction and therefore to an apologetic stance.[8] Not until 1892 did positive theology pass over to the attack with a programmatic book by Martin Kähler, a book ahead of its time and embodying a specific thesis: *The So-Called Historical Jesus and the Historic, Biblical Christ.*[9] The title of this work must be carefully examined if we wish to understand Kähler's thesis. Kähler distinguishes, on the one hand, between "Jesus" and "Christ," and, on the other hand, between "historical" (German: *historisch*) and "historic" (*geschichtlich*). "Jesus" denoted for Kähler the man of Nazareth, as the lives of Jesus had described and were describing him, while "Christ" denoted the Savior proclaimed by the church. The term "historical" meant for him the bare facts of the past, while "historic" meant that which possesses abiding significance. That is, he set against one another the so-called "historical Jesus," as the writers of the lives of Jesus had sought to reconstruct him, and the "historic, biblical Christ," as the apostles had proclaimed him.

His thesis is as follows: Only the biblical Christ can be apprehended by us, and he alone is of abiding significance for faith. Only as the Gospels portray him for us, and not as the self-styled scientific reconstructions present him, does "the undeniable impression of the fullest reality" make its impact upon us.[10] It should be noted (because it is often overlooked) that Kähler was convinced of the "reliability" of the "vivid and coherent image of a Man, an image we never fail to recognize," that confronts us in the New Testament records.[11] At first, however, Kähler's challenge went unheard; only in our time, when Rudolf Bultmann took it up and reformulated it, has it come into its own.

## Modern Critical Theology

Inaugurated by Bultmann and under his influence, a truly fascinating development has taken place in recent decades. After one hundred and fifty years of preoccupation with the historical Jesus, critical theology came to recognize that it had undertaken an impossible task; it had the courage to acknowledge this fact openly and, with banners flying, went over into the enemy camp. It turned its back on its history, endorsed Kähler's views, at least in their negative aspects, declared its preoccupation with the historical Jesus to have been an insoluble and fruitless undertaking, and withdrew into the invulnerable bastion of the *kerygma,* the proclamation about Christ.

Critical theology has based its renunciation of the historical Jesus and return to the apostolic preaching about Christ upon two considerations.

1. Sources. It points to the peculiar character of our sources. We have no writings from the hand of Jesus, such as we possess from the hand of the apostle Paul. On the contrary, we know Jesus only from the Gospels, which are not biographies but testimonies of faith. The Gospels contain a great deal of material that has been extensively edited in the course of transmission, and many legends (one need only refer to the miracle stories). All four Gospels picture Jesus as he is apprehended by the faith of the evangelists: Mark depicts the hidden Son of God; Matthew, the secret King of Israel; Luke, the Lord of the future church; and John, the self-revealing Son of God. From this material, as a hundred unavailing attempts have shown, it is not possible to construct a life of Jesus. We must free ourselves from the subjectivity of the so-called "historical Jesus research." We must draw the full consequences of the fact that we can know Jesus only as clad in the garb of myth. We must acknowledge that we cannot go behind the kerygma. If we attempt to do so, we shall find ourselves on shaky ground.

2. Easter Faith. According to critical theology, the sources have not left us entirely in the lurch. The time is past when an unscientific skepticism could doubt whether Jesus had ever lived at all. On the contrary, we can gain considerable information about Jesus himself and about his proclamation. But

what we arrive at when we analyze the sources with the tools of historical research, says critical theology, yields nothing that would be of significance for faith. For this Jesus of Nazareth was a Jewish prophet. To be sure, he was a prophet who had apprehended "the Jewish conception of God in its purity and consistency," since he demanded absolute obedience, saw humanity as totally sinful, and proclaimed divine forgiveness to people.[12] He was indeed a prophet who claimed that a person's attitude toward his word determined his attitude toward God. But, for all that, he remained within the framework of Judaism. What he preached was a more radicalized form of Old Testament, Jewish faith in God.[13] For Bultmann, the history of Jesus is part of the history of Judaism, not of Christianity.

To be sure, this Jewish prophet is of historical interest for New Testament theology, but he neither has, nor can have, significance for Christian faith, since (and here we find an astonishing thesis) Christianity first began at Easter. Here a decisive point has been reached. Who would ever think of saying that Islam began after Mohammed's death, or Buddhism after the death of the Buddha? If we accept the thesis that Christianity began at Easter with the proclamation about the risen Christ, then indeed the logical inference is that, since Jesus was only a Jewish prophet, he does not belong to Christianity. "The message of Jesus," so runs the opening sentence of Bultmann's *Theology of the New Testament*, "belongs to the presuppositions of the theology of the New Testament and is not part of that theology itself."[14] Here the plural "presuppositions" must be especially noted. It implies that the message of Jesus is one presupposition of New Testament theology among many others, and perhaps not even the decisive one. Other factors are just as important: the Easter experiences of the disciples, the messianic expectations of Judaism, and the mythology of the pagan world that provided the garment with which Jesus of Nazareth was to be clothed. The study of Jesus and his message may be very interesting and instructive for the historical understanding of the rise of Christianity, but it has no significance for faith.

These, then, are the two bases upon which modern critical theology rests its rejection of the historical Jesus. (1) We cannot write a life of Jesus because the requisite sources are lacking; and (2) what we can regard as historical is a Jewish prophet and his message, neither of which has any significance for faith. Hence it follows that our task today is not to pursue the phantom of the historical Jesus but to interpret the kerygma, that is, the message of the apostle Paul about the justification of sinners. Admittedly, the Christianity of the Pauline and Johannine communities is a specimen of the syncretism of the Hellenistic period and as such reflects the religious climate of that day.[15] But this is not an insuperable difficulty. We must demythologize the message and translate it into modern terms with the help of existentialist philosophy, for example.

Gerhard Ebeling states these ideas very bluntly when he says that revelation is not "a historical datum" nor is it "a historic event." Revelation was not accomplished and completed during the years 1–30 C.E. Rather, it continues to take place whenever the kerygma is preached; it takes place in the act of faith.[16]

In surveying this position I have outlined, I must first point out its positive aspects. Today critical research is very different from what it was in the previous (nineteenth) century. It is bent on taking the entire kerygma into account and giving it its full due. The positive significance of this new stance of critical theology is of course immense. Nevertheless, I can see very grave dangers in this position. They are these:

- We are in danger of surrendering the affirmation "the Word became flesh" and of dissolving "salvation history," God's activity in the man Jesus of Nazareth and in his message.

- We are in danger of Docetism, where Christ becomes an idea.

- We are in danger of putting the proclamation of the apostle Paul in the place of the good tidings of Jesus.

# The Crucial Significance
## of the Historical Jesus

### *The Necessity of Historical Study*

What can be said by way of criticism of the position that I have outlined? Without a doubt it is true that the dream of ever writing a biography of Jesus is over. It would be disastrous if we were unwilling to heed critical scholarship's salutary caution regarding uncritical use of the Gospels. Nevertheless, we *must* go back to the historical Jesus and his message. We cannot bypass him. Quite apart from all theological considerations, there are two circumstances that compel us to make the attempt to ascertain the character of the gospel as Jesus proclaimed it. First of all, it is the *sources* that forbid us to confine ourselves to the kerygma of the primitive church and that force us continually to raise the question of the historical Jesus and his message. Every verse of the Gospels tells us that the origin of Christianity lies not in the kerygma, not in the resurrection experiences of the disciples, not in a "Christ-idea." Every verse tells us, rather, that the origin of Christianity lies in the appearance of the man who was crucified under Pontius Pilate, Jesus of Nazareth, and in his message. I must emphasize the last words: *and his message.*

The gospel that Jesus proclaimed antedates the kerygma of the primitive community. And as uncertain as many a detail of Jesus' life may be, his message can be clearly ascertained. To be sure, the early church recounted the accounts of Jesus and his message as testimonies to its faith, and the Gospels are, to be sure, not biographies in the sense of the Greek biographies (that much we have learned). Nevertheless, there have been gross exaggerations here. It is not as though everything in the Gospels is colored and shaped by the faith of the church and the evangelists. Paul wrote earlier than all four evangelists, and he was *the* great theologian in the Gentile Christian church before the composition of the Gospels.

But Pauline terminology is discernible only here and there in the Gospels. Jesus cannot be relegated to the rank and file of an anonymous primitive community. Over and over again we come across words that unmistakably imply a situation prior to Easter. Only occasionally do we meet with traces here and there of christological overlay; and even if everything were overlaid with Christology, the study of the historical Jesus would still remain an imperative task, since the absence of primary sources should not constitute a reason for abandoning historical research.

But it is not only the sources that compel us to keep on raising the problem of the historical Jesus and his message. The kerygma, too, the preaching about Christ by the early church, leads us back from itself at every turn. For the kerygma refers to a historical event. It proclaims: God was in Christ and reconciled the world to himself. God revealed himself in an event in history. The very heart of the kerygma, that "Christ died for our sins in accordance with the scriptures" (1 Cor 15:3), represents an interpretation of a historical event: this death happened for us. But this raises the question whether this interpretation of the crucifixion of Jesus has been arbitrarily impressed upon the events, or whether there was some circumstance in the events that caused this interpretation to be attached to it.[17] In other words, we must ask: Did Jesus himself speak of his impending death, and what significance did he attach to it? The same consideration holds true for the proclamation of the resurrection; it always refers back away from itself.

The risen and exalted Christ, whom the apostles preached and to whom the Christian community prayed, has features—lineaments and traits of personality—with which the disciples were familiar, the lineaments and traits of their earthly lord. The same is true of Paul and all the rest of the preaching of the early church: they also constantly point back behind themselves. Paul fought the self-righteousness of Jewish legalism, the self-complacency of the pious and their self-glorification, against which he set the message that we are saved by faith alone, that God offers salvation, not to the righteous but to the sinner who trusts alone in His forgiveness. But just that, although couched in other terms, is the very message of Jesus.

It is clear that we cannot understand the message of Paul unless we know the message of Jesus. Whatever statements of the kerygma we may care to examine, their origins are always to be found in the message of Jesus. That the earliest church was clearly aware of this is shown by the fact that it supplemented the *kerygma* (missionary preaching) with the *didachē* (instruction for the community), which is reflected not only in the Epistles and the Book of Revelation but also in the Gospels. At no time was there a kerygma in the earliest church without didache.

This, then, is the first consideration: we *must* continually return to the historical Jesus and his message. The sources demand it; the kerygma, which refers us back away from itself, also demands it. To put it in theological terms, the incarnation implies that the story of Jesus is not only a possible subject for historical research, study, and criticism, but demands all of these. We need to know who the Jesus of history was, as well as the content of his message. We may not avoid the offense of the incarnation. And if one objects that we fail to apprehend the essential nature of faith if we make historical knowledge the object of faith, and that faith is in this way offered up to such dubious, subjective, and hypothetical study, we can only reply that God has offered up Himself. The incarnation is the self-offering of God, and to that we can only bow in assent.

Indeed, it is precisely at this point that the latest theological developments push on beyond Bultmann's theology of the kerygma. It is now generally acknowledged that the problem of the historical Jesus must be taken seriously, and thus the situation in contemporary New Testament studies is not so heterogeneous as it might seem at first sight.

## Bulwarks against Modernizing Jesus

We must venture forth on the road to the historical Jesus and his message, no matter where it may lead us. But a second point is that we *can* venture on it with confidence, nor need we fear that we are engaging in a perilous, fruitless adventure. The question arises, however, whether we may not be in danger of ending up once again with a subjective, modernized life of Jesus. Is there not a risk that we too, like the whole of the nineteenth century, unconsciously and unintentionally, may project our own theology back into Jesus of Nazareth? With regard to this risk, it must be said that it is certainly never wholly possible for the historian to divest oneself of one's own personality. We shall never be entirely able to exclude this source of danger. Nevertheless, we need not give up in despair, for our position is entirely different from that of the previous century. We are in fact better equipped. Our aims have become more modest, because the mistakes of the "classical" quest for the historical Jesus serve as warnings to us not to want to know more than we can know; that is already a point of inestimable worth. The decisive point, however, is that we today possess, if I may use a metaphor, bulwarks that will protect us from arbitrary modernizations of Jesus, which will protect us from ourselves.

Here I will content myself with suggestions and briefly indicate five aspects of the case.

1. LITERARY CRITICISM. The critical scholarship of the previous century has thrown up the first bulwark for us in the shape of the remarkable literary criticism that it developed and increasingly refined.[18] We have been taught to distinguish sources or, more correctly (since we are becoming more and more skeptical about the assumption of written sources), strands of tradition: a Markan tradition; a sayings (logia) tradition; and the special traditions of Luke, Matthew, and John. Having established this, literary criticism leads us back to the stage of oral tradition antedating our Gospels. We have, moreover, been taught to recognize the style of composition of the evangelists, and therefore to distinguish between tradition and redaction. We have been thus enabled to trace the tradition back into its pre-literary stage.

2. FORM CRITICISM. Form criticism has led us a step further back by attempting to determine the principles that governed the shaping of the material; it has thus thrown light from another side upon the creation and growth of the tradition.[19] It is a fact not sufficiently known or heeded that the essential significance of form criticism is that it has enabled us to remove a Hellenistic layer that had overlaid an earlier Palestinian tradition.

3. ANCIENT PALESTINE. We have been carried an important step further on the way back to Jesus himself by studies that disclose to us his environment and inform us about the religious climate and of Palestinian customs in his day.[20] I am referring to the study of rabbinical literature and of late Jewish apocalyptic. As one who was privileged to live in Palestine for some years, I can testify from my own experience how much light has been cast in this way upon the Gospels.[21] The importance of the study of both ancient and modern Palestine does not lie primarily in the fact that it has revealed to us how Jesus belonged to his own time; its main significance lies rather in the way in which it has helped us to realize afresh the sharpness of Jesus' opposition to the religiosity of his time. And this is the chief significance of the Dead Sea Scrolls for New Testament studies. The Essenism they disclose to us enables us to realize from their own testimony to what extent the whole of late Judaism was imbued with a passion to establish God's holy community. We can now assess more clearly than was previously possible the significance of the emphatic denial with which Jesus met all these attempts.

4. ARAMAIC. A further result of the study of the environment of Jesus has been to force upon us the necessity of studying his mother tongue. It was some seventy years ago that Gustav Dalman proved conclusively, in my estimation, that Jesus spoke Galilean Aramaic.[22] Since then the study of this dialect has been pursued but is still only in an early stage. We lack critical editions of the texts and a vocabulary of Galilean Aramaic. But the studies made

so far have already demonstrated how rewarding such meticulous philological research can be. It is only necessary to recall in how many cases one and the same saying of Jesus has been transmitted to us in different Greek forms. In most of these cases we are dealing with translation variants, which constitute a reliable aid in reconstructing the Aramaic form of the saying underlying the various versions. For example, the Lord's Prayer, the Greek renderings of which in Matthew and Luke show many divergences, can by this means be retranslated into Jesus' mother tongue with a high degree of probability (see chapter 2).

Anyone who has ever had anything to do with translations is aware that translations can never take the place of the original and will be able to assess how important it is that we should be able to get back, with a high degree of probability, to the original Aramaic underlying the Greek tradition. It must of course be remembered that the earliest Christian community spoke Aramaic too; so not every Aramaism is evidence of authenticity. At any rate, however, we are drawing nearer to Jesus himself when we succeed in rediscovering the pre-Hellenistic form of the tradition. In this connection it is of special importance to note that this kind of study reveals peculiarities in the utterances of Jesus that are without contemporary parallels. As a form of address to God, the word *'Abba'* (Father) is without parallel in the whole of late Jewish devotional literature. Similarly there is no contemporary analogy to Jesus' use of *'Amen* as an introduction to his own utterances. It may be maintained that these two characteristic features of the "actual voice" (*ipsissima vox*) of Jesus contain, in a nutshell, his message and his consciousness of his authority.[23]

5. ESCHATOLOGY. Of special significance as a bulwark against a psychological modernizing of Jesus is the rediscovery of the eschatological character of his message. It is not only that we have learned to recognize how extensively Jesus shared the conceptions of contemporary apocalyptic and made use of its language; the decisive importance of this discovery lies elsewhere. We have seen how the whole message of Jesus flowed from an awareness that God was about to break into history, an awareness of the approaching crisis, the coming judgment, and we have seen the significance of the fact that it was against this background that he proclaimed the present in-breaking in his own ministry of the kingdom of God.[24]

It is clear, then, that Jesus was no Jewish rabbi, no teacher of wisdom, no prophet, but that his proclamation of a God who was at the present moment offering a share in salvation to the despised, the oppressed, and the despairing, ran counter to all the religiosity of his time and was in truth the end of Judaism.

At the end of his book *The Quest of the Historical Jesus*, Albert Schweitzer summed up the outcome of the attempts to write a life of Jesus:

The study of the Life of Jesus has had a curious history. It set out in quest of the historical Jesus, believing that when it had found him it could bring him straight into our time as a teacher and saviour. It loosed the bands by which for centuries he had been riveted to the stony rocks of ecclesiastical doctrine, and rejoiced to see life and movement coming into the figure once more, and the historical Jesus advancing, as it seemed, to meet it. But he did not stay; he passed by our time and returned to his own.[25]

Such was the remarkable outcome of the study of the life of Jesus begun in 1778 with Reimarus. It had freed Jesus from fetters; he became a living figure, belonging to the present; he became a man of our own time. Yet he did not stay, but passed by our time and returned to his own. It became clear that he was not a man of our time, but the prophet of Nazareth, who spoke the language of the prophets of the old covenant and proclaimed the God of the old covenant. But we must now extend Schweitzer's metaphor. Jesus did not stay in his own time, but he also passed beyond his own time. He did not remain the rabbi of Nazareth, the prophet of late Judaism. He receded into the distance, entered into the dim light of Easter morning and became, as Schweitzer says in the closing paragraph of his book, the One unknown, without a name, who speaks the words, "Follow me!"[26]

## Historical Study and Jesus' Claims

If we travel the road indicated so far, threading our way amid the five protecting walls that guard us from modernizing Jesus and fashioning him in our own likeness, we are then confronted by a unique claim to authority that breaks through the bounds of the Old Testament and of Judaism. Everywhere we are confronted by this ultimate claim in the message of Jesus. That is to say, we are confronted by the same claim to faith as that with which the kerygma presents us. We must at this point reiterate one of the simplest and most obvious facts, since it is no longer obvious to all. Every sentence of the sources bears witness of this fact to us, every verse of our Gospels hammers it into us: something has happened, something unique, something that had never happened before.

The study of the history of religions has amassed countless parallels and analogies to the message of Jesus. As far as our knowledge of Pharisaic and rabbinical theology is concerned, for instance, the monumental work of Paul Billerbeck is unsurpassed and will long remain so.[27] Yet the more analogies we amass, the clearer it becomes that there are no analogies to the message of Jesus. There is no parallel to his message that God is concerned with sinners and not with the righteous, and that he grants them, here and now, a share in his kingdom. There is no parallel to Jesus' sitting down in table-fellowship with publicans and sinners. There is no parallel to the authority with which he dares to address God as *'Abba'*. Anyone who admits merely the fact—and I cannot see how it can be contradicted—that the word *'Abba'* is an authentic utterance of Jesus is (if the word is understood correctly, without watering down its meaning) thereby confronted with Jesus' claim to authority. Anyone who reads the parable of the Prodigal Son, which belongs to the bedrock of the tradition, and observes how in this parable, which describes the unimaginable goodness of divine forgiveness, Jesus justifies his table fellowship with publicans and sinners, is again confronted with the claim of Jesus to be regarded as God's representative, acting with his authority.[28]

One example after another could be cited, but if we apply the critical resources at our disposal to the study of the historical Jesus with utmost discipline and conscientiousness, the final result is always the same: we find ourselves confronted with God. The sources bear witness to this fact: A man appeared, and those who received his message were certain that they had heard the word of God. It is not as if faith were made superfluous or belittled, when exegesis shows us that behind every word and every deed of Jesus lies his claim to authority. (How could faith ever become superfluous?) Indeed, the truth of the matter is that through the words and deeds of Jesus at every turn the challenge to faith is presented. When we read the Gospels, even when we read them critically, we cannot evade this challenge. This claim to divine authority is the origin of Christianity, and therefore study of the historical Jesus and his message is no peripheral task of New Testament scholarship, a study of one particular historical problem among many others. It is *the* central task of New Testament scholarship.

## The Good News of Jesus
## and the Proclamation of the Early Church

This brings us to one final query. If it is true that the good news of Jesus in word and deed is the origin of Christianity, then it may be asked: What is the relation between the good news of Jesus and the early church's witness of faith? What is the relation between the pre-resurrection and the post-resurrection message, between the gospel and the kerygma? With regard to these questions there are two things to be said.

First, the good news of Jesus and the early church's witness of faith are inseparable from one another. Neither of these may be treated in isolation. For the gospel of Jesus remains dead history without the witness of faith by the church, which continually reiterates, affirms, and attests to this gospel afresh. Nor can the kerygma be treated in isolation either. Apart from Jesus and his gospel, the kerygma is merely the proclamation of an idea or a theory. To isolate the message of Jesus leads to Ebionitism; to isolate the kerygma of the early church leads to Docetism.[29]

And second, if, therefore, these two belong together—the gospel of Jesus and the early church's witness of faith—and if neither of these may be isolated, it is also of utmost importance to recognize (and this is decisive) that they are not both on the same level. The gospel of Jesus and the kerygma of the early church must not be placed on the same footing, but they are related to one another as call and response. The life, acts, and death of Jesus, the authoritative word of him who dared to say 'Abba', the one who with divine authority invited sinners to his table, and as the servant of God went to the cross—all this is the call of God.

The early church's witness of faith, the Spirit-led chorus of a thousand tongues, is the response to God's call. The ancient church liked to express this relationship in pictorial representations of the cosmic liturgy, in the midst of which is depicted a gigantic figure of the Crucified, toward whom, from the right and the left, there streams a countless throng on earth and in heaven. What such representations say is that Jesus of Nazareth is God's call to his creatures; confessing him is their response. This response always has a double aspect: it is praise and adoration of God and the witness to the world. It is inspired by the Spirit of God, but it does not take the place of the call. The call, not the response, is the decisive thing. The many-sided witness of the early church—of Paul, John, the Epistle to the Hebrews—must be judged in light of the message of Jesus.

Underlying our protest against the equating of the gospel and the kerygma is a concern for the concept of revelation. According to the witness of the New Testament, there is no other revelation of God but the incarnate Word. The preaching of the early church, on the other hand, is the divinely inspired witness *to* the revelation, but the church's preaching is not itself the revelation. To put it bluntly, revelation does not take place from eleven to twelve o'clock on Sunday morning. Golgotha is not everywhere; there is only *one* Golgotha, and it lies just outside the walls of Jerusalem.[30]

The doctrine of continuous revelation (*revelatio continua*) is a gnostic heresy. No, the church's proclamation is, from its earliest beginnings, not itself revelation, but it does guide toward the revelation. This, at any rate, is the way Paul conceived of the task of the kerygma when he told the Galatians that the content of his preaching had been the depiction of Christ crucified before their eyes (Gal 3:1; see 1 Cor 2:2).

Once more, according to the witness of the New Testament, the church's proclamation is not revelation, but it leads to the revelation. Jesus is Lord. The Lord is above the one who proclaims the message. For faith, there is no other authority but the Lord. The historical Jesus and his message, therefore, are not *one* presupposition among many for the kerygma, but the *sole* presupposition of the kerygma. The response, consequently, precedes the call, and the witness to the revelation presupposes the revelation. Only the Son of Man and his word can give authority to the proclamation. No one else and nothing else.

## NOTES

[1.] For a good overview of the current discussion, see Gerd Theissen and Annette Merz, *The Historical Jesus: A Comprehensive Guide*, trans. J. Bowden (Minneapolis: Fortress Press, 1998).

[2.] The Greek term *kerygma* means "proclamation." Compare Bultmann's pivotal comment: "But Christian faith did not exist until there was a Christian kerygma; i.e., a kerygma proclaiming Jesus Christ—specifically Jesus Christ the Crucified and Risen One—to be God's eschatological act of salvation," Rudolf Bultmann, *Theology of the New Testament*, 2 vols., trans. K. Grobel (New York: Scribners, 1951–55) 1.3.

3. Reimarus, *Von dem Zwecke Jesu und seiner Jünger: Noch ein Fragment des Wolfenbüttel Ungenanten* (Braunschweig, 1778; new ed., Berlin: Wever, 1788). The English translation is *Reimarus: Fragments*, ed. C. H. Talbert, trans. R. S. Fraser, Lives of Jesus Series (Philadelphia: Fortress Press, 1970).

4. *Von Reimarus zu Wrede*. [Ed.] The earlier English translation by Montgomery (1910; 410 pp.) was based on the first German edition; but the second German edition was considerably changed and expanded. A translation of this 2nd edition is now available in English (608 pp.): *The Quest of the Historical Jesus*, 1st complete ed., ed. J. Bowden (Minneapolis: Fortress Press, 2001).

5. Compare J. Leipoldt, *Vom Jesusbilde der Gegenwart: Sechs Aufsätze*, 2nd ed. (Leipzig: Dörffling & Franke, 1925). [Ed.] For contemporary treatments, see Marcus J. Borg, *Jesus in Contemporary Scholarship* (Valley Forge, Pa.: Trinity Press International, 1994); Mark Allan Powell, *Jesus as a Figure in History: How Modern Historians View the Man from Galilee* (Louisville: Westminster John Knox, 1997); William R. Herzog II, *Jesus, Justice, and the Reign of God: A Ministry of Liberation* (Louisville: Westminster John Knox, 2000).

[6.] *Parousia* is the Greek word meaning "arrival." It is used in Matthew 24:3 to signal the arrival of Christ in glory (see also 2 Cor 7:6 and Phil 1:26, referring to Titus and Paul), and it has become a technical designation in New Testament scholarship, especially associated with Mark 13, 1 Thessalonians, and Revelation 19; see Christopher Roland, "Parousia," in *ABD* 5.166–70.

7. Schweitzer, *Quest*, 327–49. [Ed.] For an analysis of Matthew 10:23, see Ulrich Luz, *Matthew 8–20*, trans. J. E. Crouch, Hermeneia (Minneapolis:

Fortress Press, 2001) 84–94. For analysis of Schweitzer's contributions, see Norman Perrin, *The Kingdom of God in the Teaching of Jesus* (London: SCM, 1963) 28–36; and Marcus Borg, "An Appreciation of Albert Schweitzer," in Schweitzer's *The Quest of the Historical Jesus*, vii–ix. For an analysis of Schweitzer's views on Matthew and Q, see James M. Robinson, "History of Q Research," in *The Critical Edition of Q*, ed. J. M. Robinson, P. Hoffmann, and J. S. Kloppenborg (Minneapolis: Fortress Press, 2000) xxxiii–xxxviii.

[8.] "Positive theology" describes an approach of some German biblical scholars in the nineteenth century. These scholars employed the methodologies of historical scholarship, but they criticized what they saw as the "negative" conclusions of more liberal scholars.

9. Martin Kähler, *The So-Called Historical Jesus and the Historic, Biblical Christ*, trans. C. E. Braaten (Philadelphia: Fortress Press, 1964). The German edition is *Der sogenannte historische Jesus und der geschichtliche, biblische Christus*, 1st ed. (Leipzig: Deichert, 1892); 2nd ed. ThBü 2 (Munich: Chr. Kaiser, 1956). [Ed.] For further analyses of Kähler's work, see Carl E. Braaten, "Martin Kähler on the Historic, Biblical Christ," in *The Historical Jesus and the Kerygmatic Christ: Essays on the Quest of the Historical Jesus*, ed. C. E. Braaten and R. Λ. Harrisville (New York: Abingdon, 1964) 79–105; Norman Perrin, *Rediscovering the Teaching of Jesus* (New York: Harper and Row, 1967) 216–18; and David Cairns, "The Motives and Scope of Historical Inquiry about Jesus," *SJT* 29 (1976) 339–44.

10. Kähler, *The So-called Historical Jesus*, 78.

11. Ibid., 89, 95.

12. Rudolf Bultmann, *Jesus and the Word*, trans. L. P. Smith and E. Huntress (New York: Scribners, 1934) 155. [Ed.] For a further analysis of Bultmann's views on the historical Jesus, see Perrin, *Rediscovering*, 218–25; and John Painter, *Theology as Hermeneutics: Rudolf Bultmann's Interpretation of the History of Jesus*, HTIBS 4 (Sheffield: Almond, 1987).

13. Bultmann, *Theology*, 1.3–26.

14. Ibid., 3. [Ed.] The published version of Bultmann's *Theology* translates his sentence using the singular "presupposition," therefore obscuring the point Jeremias makes here.

15. Rudolf Bultmann, *Primitive Christianity in its Contemporary Setting*, trans. R. H. Fuller (New York: Meridian, 1956).

16. Gerhard Ebeling, *The Problem of Historicity in the Church and Its Proclamation*, trans. G. Foley (Philadelphia: Fortress Press, 1967) 72, 73, 77. [Ed.] For a further analysis of Ebeling, see Perrin, *Rediscovering*, 227–29.

[17.] See, for example, Sam K. Williams, *Jesus' Death as Saving Event: The Background and Origin of a Concept*, HDR 2 (Missoula, Mont.: Scholars, 1975); C. F. D. Moule, *The Origins of Christology* (Cambridge: Cambridge Univ. Press,

1977) 107–26; and David Seeley, *The Noble Death: Graeco-Roman Martyrology and Paul's Concept of Salvation*, JSNTSup 28 (Sheffield: JSOT Press, 1990).

[18.] For an up-to-date treatment of the Synoptic Problem, see John S. Kloppenborg Verbin, *Excavating Q: The History and Setting of the Sayings Gospel* (Minneapolis: Fortress Press, 2000) 11–54.

[19.] For classic statements of New Testament form criticism, see Martin Dibelius, *From Tradition to Gospel*, trans. B. L. Woolf (New York: Scribners, 1934); Rudolf Bultmann, *The History of the Synoptic Tradition*, rev. ed., trans. J. Marsh (New York: Harper and Row, 1962); and William G. Doty, "The Discipline and Literature of New Testament Form Criticism," *ATR* 51 (1969) 257–321. For more recent treatments, see James L. Bailey and Lyle D. Vander Broek, *Literary Forms in the New Testament* (Louisville: Westminster John Knox, 1992); and Vernon K. Robbins, "Form Criticism," in *ABD* 2.841–44.

[20.] For treatments of first-century Palestinian society, see Joachim Jeremias, *Jerusalem in the Time of Jesus: An Investigation into Economic and Social Conditions during the New Testament Period*, trans. F. H. Cave and C. H. Cave (Philadelphia: Fortress Press, 1969); Richard A. Horsley, *Galilee: History, Politics, People* (Valley Forge, Pa.: Trinity Press International, 1995); idem, *Archaeology, History, and Society in Galilee: The Social Context of Jesus and the Rabbis* (Valley Forge, Pa.: Trinity Press International, 1996); K. C. Hanson and Douglas E. Oakman, *Palestine in the Time of Jesus: Social Structures and Social Conflicts* (Minneapolis: Fortress Press, 1998); and Bruce J. Malina, *The New Testament World: Insights from Cultural Anthropology*, 3rd ed. (Louisville: Westminster John Knox, 2001).

[21.] Jeremias lived in Palestine between the ages of ten and fifteen (approx. 1910–15); his father, Friedrich Jeremias, was the pastor/dean of Church of the Redeemer in Jerusalem.

[22.] Gustaf Dalman, *The Words of Jesus Considered in the Light of Post-Biblical Jewish Writings and the Aramaic Language*, trans. D. M. Kay (Edinburgh: T. & T. Clark, 1902; 1st German ed. 1898; 2nd ed. 1930); Matthew Black, *An Aramaic Approach to the Gospels and Acts* (Peabody, Mass.: Hendrickson, 1998); and Joseph A. Fitzmyer, "Methodology in the Study of the Aramaic Substratum of Jesus' Sayings in the New Testament," in *A Wandering Aramean: Collected Aramaic Essays*, SBLMS 25 (Missoula, Mont.: Scholars, 1979) 1–27.

[23.] *Ipsissima vox* is Latin for "actual voice." Jeremias uses this as a more general notion, standing in contrast to the more specific *ipsissima verba*, "actual words."

[24.] See Perrin, *Kingdom*; idem, *Rediscovering*, 154–206.

25. Schweitzer, *Quest*, 478.

26. Schweitzer, *Quest*, 487.

[27.] Hermann L. Strack and Paul Billerbeck, *Kommentar zum Neuen Testa-*

*ment aus Talmud und Midrasch*, 6 vols. (Munich: Beck, 1922–61). Jeremias and K. Adolph were responsible for the extensive indices comprising vols. 5 and 6.

28. See Ernst Fuchs, "The Question of the Historical Jesus," in *The Historical Jesus and the Kerygmatic Christ*, 20–21. [Ed.] See also Jeremias, *The Parables of Jesus*, rev. ed., trans. S. H. Hooke (New York: Scribners, 1972) 128–32.

[29.] The Ebionites—according to Irenaeus, Tertullian, and others—were a sect of early Christians who emphasized the keeping of the law, the Gospel of Matthew, and the natural birth of Jesus; see Joseph A. Fitzmyer, "The Qumran Scrolls, the Ebionites and Their Literature," in *Essays on the Semitic Background of the New Testament*, SBLSBS 5 (Missoula, Mont.: Scholars, 1974) 435–48. Docetism was a perspective (particularly in the second and third centuries) rather than a group, which considered Jesus' humanity and suffering to be only apparent, not real; it takes its name from the Greek verb *dokeō* ("seem," "appear"); see Gregory J. Riley, *One Jesus, Many Christs: How Jesus Inspired Not One True Christianity But Many* (San Francisco: HarperSanFrancisco, 1997; reprint, Minneapolis: Fortress Press, 2000) 125–38.

30. Paul Althaus, *Fact and Faith in the Kerygma of Today*, trans. D. Cairns (Philadelphia: Muhlenberg, 1960) 58.

# 2

# The Sermon on the Mount

## The Problem

What is the meaning of the Sermon on the Mount? This is a profound question and one that affects not only our preaching and teaching but also, when we really face up to it, the very roots of our existence. Since the very beginning of the church, it has been a question with which all Christians have had to grapple, not only the theologians among them, and in the course of the centuries a whole range of answers has been given to it. In what follows I propose to discuss three of these answers.

### Perfectionism

The first answer to the question of the meaning of the Sermon on the Mount is given by what we may call the perfectionist conception. This says: In the Sermon on the Mount Jesus tells his disciples what he requires of them. He unfolds the will of God for them since this should determine their way of life. One only needs to consider the six antitheses, in which the old and the new conceptions of the will of God are contrasted with each other. "You have heard . . . but I say to you . . ." (Matt 5:21, 22). Here one clear instruction is followed by another; and so it continues in Matthew 6 and further in Matthew 7.

From this conception, however, one thing follows, and it is to the merit of Hans Windisch, the late professor of New Testament at Halle, Germany, that he drew this consequence with ruthless honesty in his book *The Meaning of the Sermon on the Mount.*[1] If it is right that Jesus gives simple commandments in the Sermon on the Mount, and if he expected his disciples to keep them, then we must ask: Is this not legalistic thinking? Is this not ethical perfectionism? Windisch answers: Yes, it is so. Let us be honest; let us free ourselves once and for all from that idealistic and Paulinizing exegesis! We must admit that the ethic of the Sermon on the Mount is every bit as much an obedience ethic as is the ethic of the Old Testament. Nothing is said in the Sermon about the inability of humans to do good; nor is there anything to be read here of the office of Jesus as mediator or of the redemption through his blood. What stands in the Sermon on the Mount is, from the point of view of Paul, Martin Luther, or John Calvin, complete heresy, for this is perfectionism, this is righteousness by works, this is law and not gospel.

The Sermon on the Mount, Windisch concludes, stands fully in the context of the Old Testament and of Judaism. For this is what the Old Testament tirelessly repeats: Obey, then you will live! In exactly the same way the central theme of the theology of Judaism at the time of Jesus was the inexorable nature of the law of God. In the Talmud we can read, admittedly side by side with a great deal of casuistry, the same condemnation of lust, hate, and vengeance that is found in the Sermon on the Mount.

We also find in the Talmud the Golden Rule of Matthew 7:12. "In everything do to others as you would have them do to you; for this is the law and the prophets," says Jesus. In the Talmud this saying is found in the context of the well-known story of Hillel (20 B.C.E.) and the Gentile who was prepared to become a proselyte. This Gentile had gone first to Shammai, Hillel's contemporary and rival, and demanded of him that he should teach him the whole law in the time in which he could stand on one leg. Shammai, who was a carpenter, had taken his yardstick and driven him out. Now he came to Hillel with his demand, and Hillel answered him: Yes, I can do it. I can indeed teach you the whole law in the time in which you can stand on one leg—and then he said: "What is hateful to you, do not do to anyone else. The whole law is contained in this sentence. All the rest is only commentary."[2] It is the Stoic teaching of an unwritten law that Hillel took up, when, with what was amazing candor and a magnificent inner freedom for a rabbi, he ventured to make the bold statement: The Golden Rule is the heart of the Torah; all other precepts are only expositions of it.

Similarly in Matthew 7:12 we find the Golden Rule with the addition (omitted in Luke 6:31, probably in view of the Gentile-Christian readers): "This is the law and the prophets." To be sure, the Golden Rule is given by Jesus in a positive form and by Hillel in a negative one. That is a great difference. Hillel says: "You shall not do harm to your neighbor"; but with Jesus it is a case of: "The love that you yourself would experience, you should show to your neighbor." To give love is far more than to refrain from harming. Despite this significant difference, a relationship between the sayings of Jesus and Hillel here is very probable.

Must we not then go on to say: What Jesus teaches in the Sermon on the Mount is every bit as much perfectionist legalism as is the teaching of Hillel? I am afraid that the conception that Windisch represents is by and large the most widely accepted conception of the Sermon on the Mount in contemporary thought, represented for example in a statement such as: Here Jesus is making most extreme demands, although he knows that nobody can completely fulfill them; but he hopes to bring people to the point where they exert themselves seriously in an attempt to attain a part of them.

What are we to say concerning this first conception? Well, there is a real element of validity in it. The Sermon on the Mount is certainly concerned with the will of God, and we find in it concrete, hard and fast demands. Jesus says what he really expects from his disciples: "Everyone then who hears these words of mine and does them is like a wise man" (Matt 7:24). It is also quite valid to say that Jesus is firmly rooted in his own time, or rather that both Jesus and late Judaism are firmly rooted in the Old Testament. We may not lightly ignore the common ground between Jesus and the Judaism of his day, as can happen if we content ourselves with a caricature of that Judaism. But there are nonetheless differences, great differences, between the demands of Jesus and the ethic of late Judaism. I would indicate four such differences:

1. Certainly a good deal of what is found in the Sermon on the Mount can also be found in the Talmud, not merely the Golden Rule. Julius Wellhausen has deliberately overstated the case thus: Everything that is to be found in the Sermon on the Mount is also to be found in the Talmud—and a great deal more. That is exactly the case, that in the Talmud "a great deal more" is to be found, and that one must seek the grain among a great deal of chaff, the scanty golden grain that may be compared with the words of the Sermon on the Mount.

2. The comparison between the Sermon on the Mount and the Talmud also reveals that, significantly, it is the decisive sayings in the Sermon for which there are no parallels in the Talmud. One seeks there in vain for parallels to the blessing of the poor, forbidding divorce, turning the cheek, the momentous "love your enemies," the joy of repentance (Matt 5:3, 32, 39, 44; 6:16-18), and many others.

3. It is much more the case that the Sermon on the Mount as a whole (and especially Matt 5:21-48; 6:1-18) stands in conscious and decisive contrast to rabbinical-Pharisaic piety.

4. Jesus even goes so far as to set his teaching over against that of the Torah. The criticism that is implied in the antitheses to the Torah would be, in the eyes of his contemporaries, blasphemy against the divine law, and as such the decisive break with Jewish piety.

It is not, therefore, so simple a matter to set the Sermon on the Mount in the context of late Judaism. Now, naturally, Windisch is conscious of this and therefore says: What we find in the Matthean composition as a whole, as well as in the separate sayings, is not simply the ethic of late Judaism, but a refined,

humanized, radicalized, simplified, concentrated Judaism that finds its fulfillment in the confession of Jesus.[3] We could continue to suggest similar modify-
ing adjectives, but this would not bring us to the heart of the matter with
regard to the Sermon on the Mount. The fact is that Jesus was not a teacher of
the law, or a preacher of wisdom, such as could be found among his contemporaries; his message burst the bounds of late Judaism.

## Impossible Ideal

We now turn to a second answer to the question of the meaning of the Sermon
on the Mount. It is the answer that has been given by Lutheran orthodoxy: the
theory of the impossible ideal.[4] This has not only played a great part in past
centuries; even today it has numerous supporters. With this conception of the
meaning of the Sermon, we move out of the superficiality of the theory that we
discussed first and into deeper realms. The second conception says: When we
read the Sermon on the Mount earnestly, we are of necessity moved to
despair. Jesus demands that we should free ourselves from anger; even an
unfriendly word is to be reckoned as murder. Jesus demands a chastity that
extends even to the avoidance of an impure look. Jesus demands absolute
veracity and that we should love our enemies. Who lives like this? Who can
live like this? Who can fulfill these demands? This is the point of departure for
the theory of the impossible ideal. It says: It is a great mistake to regard the
Sermon on the Mount as capable of being fulfilled; these sayings of Jesus cannot be fulfilled, and Jesus knows this.

What is Jesus' intention then in teaching these things? The answer of the
theory of the impossible ideal is that it can best be understood when these
demands are viewed through eyes that have been sharpened by what Paul has
to say about the law. The law, says Paul, has not been given that it may lead to
life. It is not law that saves, but faith. Law awakens the consciousness of sin;
law provokes transgression. The law is preparation for the gospel (*praeparatio
evangelica*) in that it reveals to humans their impotence; by driving them to
despair it opens their eyes to the wonder of the mercy of God. It is exactly the
same with the Sermon on the Mount, and this was the intention of Jesus. He
wanted to bring his hearers to the consciousness that they cannot, in their
own strength, fulfill the demands of God. He intends to lead people, through
the experience of their failure, to despair of themselves. His demands are
designed to shatter our self-reliance; nothing else is intended. The Sermon on
the Mount, according to this second theory, is *Mosissimus Moses,* to take a
phrase from Martin Luther; it is Moses quadrupled, Moses multiplied to the
highest degree. If the first conception sees in the Sermon on the Mount a perfectionist law, this second discovers in it a *propaedeutic law,* that is, a law with
the purpose of preparing people for salvation.

Again, in my opinion, we must say emphatically that there is a real element of validity here. On the one hand it is a valid emphasis that the demands of Jesus are to be taken seriously and may not be trifled with, and on the other hand our poverty is also taken seriously. But what does the actual text of the Sermon say? Where in the Sermon does one find even a hint upon which such an interpretation could be based? Certainly there are some sayings that seem to bear the stamp of the impossibility of fulfillment, for example: "If your right eye causes you to sin, tear it out and throw it away . . . and if your right hand causes you to sin, cut it off and throw it away" (Matt 5:29-30). But one cannot build a theory on sayings such as these, for this is a paradoxical exaggeration such as we often find in Eastern sayings, just as a saying like that of the speck and the log (Matt 7:4-5) is paradoxical picture-language. Such language does not justify the conclusion that Jesus was deliberately stating an impossible ideal.

Nowhere in the Sermon on the Mount is there a clear statement that points unmistakably in this direction and upon which such a theory could be built. Nowhere is there to be found, as there is in Paul, reflection upon the inability of people to fulfill God's will. Rather, Jesus astonishingly expected his disciples to do what he commanded. He addresses himself throughout to the will of people. The conclusion of the Sermon shows this especially clearly: the four groups of pictures of the narrow and wide gate, of the sound and bad trees, of the people standing before God's throne at the final judgment, and of the building of a house on rock and sand (7:13-27). When the waves of the last judgment beat upon the rock, then the person will stand firm who "hears these words of mine and does them," and only that one. The instructions of the Sermon apply to everyone who is a disciple of Jesus. They direct his way to the narrow gate, to the reign of God. So we must reject also the theory of the impossible ideal. It is, in fact, a classic example of what the consequences are when one interprets Jesus in the light of Paul, instead of interpreting Paul in the light of Jesus. It is Paulinizing exegesis, and that means it is eisegesis.

## Interim Ethic

Finally, there is a third understanding of the Sermon that deserves mention, that which understands it as an interim ethic. This interpretation was first developed at the end of the last century by Johannes Weiss,[5] and it is also to be found in the works of Albert Schweitzer.[6] Both of these authors wrote in the era of the belief in progress and of "culture Protestantism," when the preaching of Jesus was viewed as a culture-ethic. Against this background they developed their eschatological interpretation of the gospel. They claimed that Jesus does not preach a long-term culture-ethic, but rather his demands are rooted in the terrible earnestness of the hour. The supreme crisis is at hand. The time of decision has come. God has given humanity a last opportunity for repentance and decision before the waves of the flood break once more into history, before the judgment upon Sodom and Gomorrah is repeated. And the main source for this new and radically eschatological view of the preaching of Jesus is the Sermon on the Mount.

For the Sermon contains, according to the tenets of "thoroughgoing eschatology," exceptional laws, laws valid only for the time of crisis.[7] It is, so to speak, a form of martial law declared in the last decisive phase of a total war. The Sermon was preached to people who knew that they were standing under a dangerously leaning wall that might at any moment come tumbling down upon them; to people who found themselves in the position of a dying man who knows that he has only very little time left. This means that the words of the Sermon on the Mount are a challenge to most exceptional effort in the face of catastrophe, a last call to repentance before the End. Because the situation is so critical, Jesus demands of his disciples that they burn all bridges behind them; they must have no ties left at all to the world. Let the dead bury the dead! All possessions are equally valueless in this catastrophic situation; they must be cast away so that they do not bind the disciples of Jesus. Even the right of self-defense may play no part in this last hour (Matt 5:38-48). In this hour Jesus demands unprecedented commitment, even to the love of enemies. All these are heroic commands, valid only for the short period before the End in which unheard-of sacrifices must be made. In short, the Sermon on the Mount offers an *interim-ethic*.

Once more it must be said emphatically that here again there is an element of validity, in fact, an element of decisive importance. Here we have really come a step nearer to the heart of the matter, for the whole preaching of Jesus is in fact directed to the imminent End. This lies unexpressed behind every word that he says, even those of the Sermon on the Mount. He actually brings God's last word. One's attitude to this last word of God is a matter of life and death; the hell of which Jesus speaks (Matt 5:22, 29, 30) is not something that lies in the distant future, but a threat that is drawing near to his hearers. The dynamic of eschatology lies beyond every word of Jesus, and here nothing may be explained away or rendered harmless. God gives one last respite; it is pure compassion on the part of God that allows the fig tree to stand for one year more (Luke 13:6-9). This is something that we can understand better than could the people of the late nineteenth century.

But here too we have questions. A straining toward the maximum possible effort is exactly what we do not find in the Sermon on the Mount. It is not an ethic of the death-hour nor the utterance of a voice from a world on the brink of catastrophe. Where the mistake lies can be seen from a statement by Johannes Weiss concerning the commands to abjure vengeance and to love one's enemies, which in his opinion are the two classical examples of this exceptional eschatological law. He says: "For such a love the normal abilities of people are insufficient. There must be a special impetus, an intensification and heightening of the spiritual powers, such as is promised to the disciples for the times of stress and strain."[8] But nothing of this "special impetus," of this "heightening of spiritual powers," appears in the text. Jesus is no fanatical enthusiast; his ethic is not an expression of anxiety in the face of catastrophe. Rather, the dominating thing for Jesus is something quite different: knowledge of the presence of salvation. Here is to be found the great difference from the ethics of Pharisaism and of apocalyptic. In the case of Jesus the decisive accent is not upon human effort, but upon the fact that the salvation of God is here. Jesus quite certainly did not proclaim an exceptional law for a short interim period; his words have validity not only up to the End, but also after it (Mark 13:31).

The three attempts at a solution that I have discussed, for all the great differences between them, have nonetheless one thing in common: all three of them regard the Sermon on the Mount as law, and in this regard it makes no difference in the end whether this law is more nearly defined as perfectionistic, as a tutoring into salvation, or as an interim ethic. Every legalistic understanding of the Sermon puts Jesus within the realm of late Judaism. The first conception makes him a teacher of the law, the second a preacher of repentance, the third an apocalypticist. But was he any of these things?

## THE ORIGINS OF THE SERMON ON THE MOUNT

How do we find our way out of this impasse? We can find help by considering the results of the most recent research into the origins of the Sermon on the Mount by means of literary and form criticism. Four essential observations must be taken into account.

### The Structure of Matthew

The evangelist Matthew wrote his gospel about 75–80 C.E. He used as his basis the Gospel of Mark, but he added very considerably to this basis, especially in regard to sayings, for he had at his disposal many sayings of Jesus not found in Mark. He built these sayings into the structure of the Markan gospel at suitable points; for example, he expands the three parables from Mark 4 into a more extensive parabolic discourse now containing seven parables in Matthew 13. So we now find in Matthew's Gospel five great discourses: the Sermon on the Mount (Matthew 5–7); the Mission Discourse (Matthew 10); the Parable Discourse (Matthew 13); guidance for conduct in the community (Matthew 18); and finally the great Farewell Discourse in Jerusalem (Matthew

23–25). That Matthew has in fact deliberately constructed his Gospel in this manner is a conclusion to be drawn with complete certainty from the fact that he ends each of these five discourses with one and the same formula (with minor variations): "And when Jesus had finished these sayings . . ." (7:28; 11:1; 13:53; 19:1; 26:1).[9]

The possibility has been suggested that Matthew, in giving these five discourses of Jesus, has been influenced by the five books of Moses; that in this way he intended to present Jesus as the proclaimer of a new Pentateuch, as the second Moses, as the one who establishes the Messianic torah. But here we need to be cautious. The detailed explanation that Matthew gives for his use of the number fourteen in the genealogy of Jesus (1:17) leaves the impression that he would have drawn attention to the fact if he had intended the number of five discourses to have such a symbolic significance. But a different conclusion may well be drawn with some degree of certainty. In chapters 5–7 Matthew records the Sermon on the Mount as the first discourse and then goes on (in chaps. 8–9) to add a collection of miracle stories. He intends therefore to portray Jesus as the Messiah in word and as the Messiah in deed. Both belong together: word and deed. Wherever the Spirit of God is manifested, it is manifested in this combination of word and deed; never simply in words and never simply in deeds. So in bringing together chapters 5–7 and 8–9, Matthew intends to express one thing: Jesus is one in whom the spirit of God is manifested in its fullness.

### The Lukan Parallel

We take a step further when we observe that the Sermon on the Mount has an equivalent in the Gospel of Luke, namely, the Sermon on the Plain in Luke 6:20-49. The Sermon on the Plain also begins with the beatitudes; it then goes on to sayings that are also found in the Sermon on the Mount: on love for enemies, on turning the other cheek, the Golden Rule, the exhortation to be merciful (Luke 6:27, 29, 31, 36), and so on. And it concludes, as does the Sermon on the Mount, with the parable of the house-builder. But the Sermon on the Plain is very much shorter than the Sermon on the Mount, and from this we must conclude that in the Lukan Sermon on the Plain we have an earlier form of the Sermon on the Mount.

### An Underlying Aramaic Version

When we go on to compare the Sermon on the Mount with the Sermon on the Plain, we notice at once that there are considerable differences in phraseology. The very first sentence in Luke reads, "Blessed are you who are poor" (second person, 6:20). In Matthew, on the other hand, it is "Blessed are the poor in spirit" (third person, 5:3). Similar variations in wordings are to be found in

practically every verse. These are sometimes to be attributed to the evangelists themselves; for example, in Matthew 5:3 the addition "in spirit" could
come from Matthew.

But in the vast majority of cases it is a matter of translation variants; one
and the same Aramaic text has been translated into Greek in two different
ways. We may take as an example the conclusion of the beatitudes (Matt 5:12;
par. Luke 6:23). The differences here are as follows:

> Matthew: "Rejoice (present imperative) and be glad"
> Luke:    "Rejoice (aorist imperative) in that day and leap for joy"
>
> Matthew: "for your reward is great in the heavens (plural)"
> Luke:    "for behold, your reward is great in heaven (singular)"
>
> Matthew: "for so they persecuted the prophets who were before you"
> Luke:    "for that is what their ancestors did to the prophets."

These differences are doubtless due to an Aramaic tradition that has been
rendered into Greek in different ways. This is especially clear in the case of the
very last words, where the Aramaic original has been understood by one
translator as an apposition (Matthew: "who were before you"), and by the
other as subject (Luke: "their ancestors"). With this observation, that an Aramaic tradition underlies the Sermon on the Mount and the Sermon on the
Plain, we have already moved a considerable distance behind the Sermon on
the Mount. Matthew wrote it around 75–80 C.E.; the Aramaic Sermon on the
Plain belongs to the first decades after Jesus' death.[10]

## Compositional Issues

We must still take one further step. When we look closely at the Lukan Sermon on the Plain it is noticeable that the address in it constantly varies
between the second person plural and singular. At the beginning we have the
plural: "Blessed are you who are poor, for yours is the kingdom of God," "Love
your enemies"; but then suddenly in Luke 6:29-30 the singular occurs: "If
anyone strikes you on the cheek, offer the other also." The plural follows
again in vv. 31-38, then the third person, and then again the singular in vv. 41-
42, and so on. From this the conclusion follows that the Sermon on the Plain
is a grouping together of separate sayings of Jesus that were originally spoken
on different occasions—just as the parables of Matthew 13 were originally
quite separately delivered and only later brought together into one discourse. The same is true of the Sermon on the Mount, which offers us a version of the Sermon on the Plain further expanded by the addition of still more
sayings of Jesus.[11]

We can demonstrate this compositional character of the two sermons through specific examples. Luke preserves for us a tradition with regard to the situation out of which two sections of the Sermon on the Mount arose. The first is the saying concerning the narrow gate/door (Matt 7:13-14). According to Luke, the occasion for Jesus' coining this particular image was a question from an unnamed individual concerning the number of the saved: "Lord, will only a few be saved?" Instead of giving an answer to this question, Jesus says: "Strive to enter through the narrow door" (Luke 13:23-24). The other saying in the Sermon on the Mount for which Luke has preserved a tradition with regard to the original situation is the Lord's Prayer. Jesus was praying alone and the disciples came to him and made their request: "Lord, teach us to pray, as John taught his disciples" (Luke 11:1).

We have, therefore, in the Sermon on the Mount, a composition of originally isolated sayings of Jesus. Sometimes, although by no means always, they consist of a single sentence. Each one of these sayings of Jesus, as we must envisage them, is the summary of something like a sermon by Jesus, or the essence of a piece of his teaching, that could have taken the form of question and answer and have lasted for a whole day, or it may have been the result of a dispute with his opponents. These isolated sayings were first gathered together in the form of an Aramaic Sermon on the Plain, out of which the Greek Sermon on the Plain in Luke and the Greek Sermon on the Mount in Matthew have in turn developed.

If I may express it in the form of a picture: We have learned to differentiate between the *edifice* of the Sermon on the Mount, which was built in several stages, and the *bricks* out of which the whole was built. We must therefore look at these two things separately: first the edifice as a whole, as we have it today, and then the individual bricks out of which it is built.

## THE SERMON ON THE MOUNT
## AS AN EARLY CHRISTIAN CATECHISM

The result, then, of our investigation up to this point is that the Sermon on the Mount is no more the record of a continuous sermon by Jesus than is the Parable Discourse in Matthew 13, but rather a collection of Jesus' sayings. For what purpose was this collection made? How was it arrived at?

Here it is helpful to call to mind a result of the work of C. H. Dodd, who made the fundamental observation that everywhere in the very earliest period of Christianity there were two forms of preaching, namely, proclamation (Greek: *kerygma*) and teaching (*didachē*).[12] These two conceptions are unfortunately always being confused with each other, although each of them refers to something quite different—in the Pauline usage at any rate.

Proclamation (*kerygma*) is the missionary preaching to Jews and Gentiles. The content of the missionary preaching was the message concerning the crucified and risen Lord and his return. The oldest statement of the kerygma is to be found in 1 Corinthians 15:3-5: Jesus died for our sins in accordance with the scriptures and was buried. God raised him on the third day in accordance with the scriptures, and he appeared to Cephas, then to the Twelve. Thus the kerygma is the proclamation of Christ, the message that he has redeemed us and is our peace.

To be differentiated from the kerygma is the didache, the teaching, the preaching to the congregation. The kerygma is directed outward, but the didache is directed inward. Every service of worship begins with the didache. In Acts 2:42 we have, in my opinion, a representation of the course of an early Christian service of worship. It consisted of four parts. It began with (1) the teaching (*didachē*) of the apostles; followed by (2) the fellowship (which we must probably understand as table-fellowship); after this came (3) the breaking of the bread, the Eucharist; and finally (4) the prayers. The instruction came at the beginning of the worship, and for this we have also numerous other examples.

What is, then, the content of the didache in contrast to the kerygma? Dodd answers in his work: ethical instruction, that is, instructions for Christian conduct of life. This is, of course, correct. But a proviso to this may be suggested, insofar as Dodd's definition of the didache as an ethical instruction is somewhat too narrow. The didache is not to be understood only as a kind of outer ring around the kerygma, but rather the kerygma itself was constantly repeated in these instructions to the congregation. The didache included, therefore, (1) the content of the kerygma and (2) that in which the congregation must be instructed; also much more, as for example, teaching concerning the sacraments and the last things (Heb 6:2), and also scriptural proof texts and information concerning the life of Jesus.[13]

We have many examples in the New Testament that help us to imagine the general form of such didache. For instance, in Matthew 6:5-15 and Luke 11:1-13 we find two *didachai* (instructions) of very different character, namely, two examples of instruction in prayer. When one considers first the constituent parts of the Matthean instruction in prayer, and then those of the Lukan, one sees at once the differences between the two. The Matthean instruction consists of four sayings: When you pray, you must not be like the hypocrites, who make a public show of their prayers (Matt 6:5-6); when you pray, do not heap up empty phrases (6:7-8); take the Lord's Prayer as an example of prayer that does not heap up empty phrases (6:9-13); and when you pray, then you should also forgive (6:14-15).

Like the Matthean, the Lukan prayer didache (Luke 11:1-13) also consists of four parts. First, Jesus is petitioned, "Teach us to pray," and he responds to this request by teaching the disciples the Lord's Prayer (11:1-4). Then in the parable of the friend at midnight they are taught not to give up in prayer, even when their prayer is not immediately answered (11:5-8). This is followed by the renewed instruction: Ask, and God will grant it you (11:9-10). The conclusion is given in the picture of the father who does not fail to give gifts to his son (11:11-13).

We can see that the Matthean didache is directed to people who come from a world in which they had learned to pray, but in which there was the danger of a misuse of prayer. Beyond question, we have here before us a Jewish-Christian didache.[14] The Lukan prayer didache, on the other hand, is directed to people who must learn to pray and who must be encouraged in prayer. We may see in this a Gentile-Christian instruction in prayer. The Sermon on the Mount as a whole is, together with the Epistle of James, the classical example of an early Christian didache.

Having made this much clear, we now go on to ask if we can say anything about the purpose for which this didache was composed, identifying its *Sitz im Leben*.[15] We must, therefore, consider its content carefully. The Sermon on the Mount has a very clear construction. Its theme is stated in Matthew 5:20: "For I tell you, unless your righteousness exceeds that of the scribes and Pharisees, you will never enter the kingdom of heaven." The customary interpretation tends to equate the scribes and Pharisees here. But in fact they are two quite different groups. The scribes are the theological teachers who have had some years of education. The Pharisees, on the other hand, are not theologians, but rather groups of pious laymen from every part of the community—traders, craftspersons, professionals; only their leaders were theologians.[16] According to Josephus, there were six thousand Pharisees in Palestine in the first century c.e.

Having noted the difference between the scribes and the Pharisees, we can see that Matthew 5:20 speaks of three kinds of righteousness, and this corresponds exactly to the construction of the Sermon on the Mount: it deals consecutively with the righteousness of the theologians, of the pious laymen, and of the disciples of Jesus. After the introduction (Matt 5:3-19) and the thematic sentence (5:20), the first part of the Sermon deals with the controversy concerning the interpretation of scripture between Jesus and the theologians (the six great antitheses in Matt 5:21-48). As the second part, there follows his controversy with the righteousness of the Pharisees, for almsgiving, the keeping of the three hours of prayer, and representative fasting on behalf of Israel are characteristics of these pious groups of laymen (6:1-18). The concluding section (6:19—7:27) develops the new righteousness of the disciples of Jesus. The theme of this three-part didache is therefore the way of life of Christians as distinct from that of their Jewish contemporaries.

We have in the Sermon on the Mount a composition of words of Jesus, brought together on the basis of parenetic considerations,[17] and we may conclude that its original function was in catechetical instruction (pre-baptismal).

In Luke 6:20-49 this catechism is designed for Gentile-Christians, and in Matthew 5–7 for Jewish-Christians. If in this way we have rightly determined the *Sitz im Leben* of the Sermon on the Plain and the Sermon on the Mount, then there follows a quite simple but decisively important conclusion. If the Sermon on the Mount is a catechism for baptismal candidates or newly baptized Christians, then it was preceded by something else. It was preceded by the proclamation of the gospel; and it was preceded by conversion, by a being overpowered by the Good News.

## THE INDIVIDUAL SAYINGS OF JESUS

Having considered the Sermon on the Mount as a whole, we turn finally to the individual sayings of Jesus, which are the bricks out of which the whole building has been constructed. We have already seen that in the very earliest period these were passed on as isolated sayings (Greek: *logia*). Here we find a very complex picture. The logia that have been brought together in the Sermon belong to very different form-critical categories.

There are statements by Jesus concerning himself, such as "I have come to fulfill [the law and the prophets]" (Matt 5:17); as the last messenger of God, who brings the revelation to its completion, Jesus is the proclaimer of the final will of God. In the antitheses (5:21-48), Jesus' consciousness of his mission is strongly portrayed. Schniewind has rightly stressed the fact further that the beatitudes are concealed testimonies by Jesus to himself as the savior of the poor, the sorrowing, and so on.[18] Matthew 5:18 also belongs to the category of Jesus' witness to himself, that is, if this saying refers originally to the prophecies of the passion in the Old Testament, then not an iota, not a dot, will pass from the prophecies until all is accomplished.

A second category is formed by the crisis-sayings, which speak of the imminent judgment, such as Matthew 5:25-26 (reconciliation before it is too late); Matthew 7:21-23 (before the judgment seat of God what matters is not having said "Lord, Lord," but having done God's will); Matthew 7:24-27 (the flood threatens). Then we must mention the controversy-sayings against the scribes (5:21-28) and against the Pharisees (6:1-18); some other sayings, as for example the speck and the log (7:3-5), may also have originally been controversy-sayings.

Further, we find mission-sayings. To this group probably belongs the long section in 6:25-34, which forbids anxiety for oneself and was very possibly originally addressed to the departing missionaries, who were to learn to depend entirely upon God.[19]

Finally—and this was the major category—we read Jesus' instructions concerning the manner of life of his disciples in the Sermon on the Mount. Here the six antitheses are to be mentioned again; one always thinks of them first when talking about the Sermon on the Mount. In them Jesus regulates one aspect of life after another: the proper attitude to a brother and to women and marriage, truthfulness in speech, and behavior with regard to an enemy (5:21-48). Furthermore, the sayings address the appropriate way regarding almsgiving, prayer, and fasting (6:1-18); the instruction to let the light shine (5:16); and many others.

When we consider the sayings and groups of sayings independently, especially those directed to the disciples, we observe again what we noted at the conclusion of our third section: we notice very quickly that we can only rightly understand the individual saying when we presuppose in each case that it was preceded by something else.

Let me demonstrate this with five examples. The short sentence, "You are the light of the world" (Matt 5:14), which compares the disciples with the sun, makes no sense when taken by itself. Can it really be said of these people, whose weaknesses and failures the evangelists do not extenuate, that they are the light that illuminates the world? The comparison becomes immediately meaningful, however, when we presuppose a previous, unexpressed sentence: "I am the light of the world" (John 8:12).

As a second example, Matthew 6:15 may be mentioned: "But if you do not forgive others, neither can [translating the Aramaic imperfect here] your Father forgive your trespasses." If we take this saying by itself, then it seems as if the law of reciprocity may be applied to the relationship between God and humanity, as in a commercial bargain. The same saying is found, however, in one other place in Matthew's Gospel, namely, as the conclusion to the parable of the unmerciful servant: "So my heavenly Father will also do to every one of you, if you do not forgive your brother from your heart" (Matt 18:35). Here we see especially clearly that this second demand was preceded by something else. It was preceded by the great debt cancellation of which the parable of the unmerciful servant speaks. Thus the demand of God that we also forgive is no longer like a commercial bargain but is an obvious foregone conclusion. "So much, you unmerciful servant, has God forgiven you; ought you not to have forgiven the little debt?"

A third example is offered by the saying on divorce (Matt 5:31-32). This was for contemporaries an extremely harsh saying, for the Jewish divorce law was regarded as a great step forward. The letter of divorce had, after all, the intention of protecting the woman, who as a divorcee was without protection. The letter gave her the right to seek the protection of another man. Jesus' rejection of divorce must have seemed harsh, not only because it cancelled out a Jewish step forward, but still more because it expressed a criticism of the Torah (Deut 24:1). This criticism of the Torah can only be properly understood if we set the rejection of divorce in the context of the discussion of divorce (Mark 10:2-12), in the course of which Jesus' opponents rely upon Moses while Jesus goes back to the creation story. The rejection of divorce is therefore preceded by the proclamation that the time of the law has run out, because the time of salvation is beginning, the time in which the original will of God, the pure paradise-will of God, is valid.

As a fourth example, I would name the command to love one's enemies (Matt 5:44-45) the hardest of commandments: "But I say to you, love your enemies and pray for those who persecute you, so that you may be children of your Father in heaven; for he makes his sun rise on the evil and on the good, and sends rain on the righteous and the unrighteous." Again something has preceded the demand of Jesus: the message of the heavenly Father, which runs like a red thread through the whole Sermon on the Mount, and of his unbounded goodness.

As a last example, we may take the saying concerning turning the other cheek as an often misunderstood saying: "You have heard it said, 'An eye for an eye and a tooth for a tooth.' But I say to you, do not go to law [this is the correct translation] against an evildoer. But if anyone strikes you on the right cheek, turn the other also" (Matt 5:38-39). The introduction, "You have heard it said . . ." immediately tells Jesus' audience something quite concrete, namely, that Jesus is now concerning himself with the civil law. The so-called *lex talionis* (law of retaliation: "an eye for an eye") was of course no longer literally applied at the time of Jesus, but it did form the foundation for the whole civil law. It was used to establish the principle that the degree of punishment should correspond to the extent of the offense. In contrast to this, Jesus says to his disciples: In the matter of legal protection through the civil law, I forbid you to make a complaint when you are offended. And as an example he chose a particularly grievous offense. Striking a person on the right cheek—a blow with the back of the hand—is still today in the East the insulting blow. But then Jesus—and this is very important for the understanding of this matter— is not speaking of a simple insult; it is much more the case of a quite specific insulting blow: the blow given to Jesus' disciples as heretics. It is true that this is not specifically stated, but it follows from the observation that in every instance where Jesus speaks of insult, persecution, anathema, dishonor to the disciples, he is concerned with outrages that arise because of discipleship itself. If you are dishonored as a heretic, says Jesus, then you should not go to law about it; rather, you should show yourselves to be truly my disciples by the way in which you bear the hatred and the insult, overcome the evil, forgive the injustice.

Again, something preceded all this: the act of becoming a follower of Jesus and of publicly confessing allegiance to him, through which the fanatical hate is first provoked. It is possible that we can be even more precise in our formulation of what preceded if we ask the question: How did Jesus come to take this particular matter of the blow on both cheeks as his example? It could naturally be that there had been an actual instance of one of his disciples having been insulted in this way. But it is perhaps much more important to note that there is but one passage in the whole of the Old Testament that speaks of the voluntary endurance of a blow on both cheeks. This is Isaiah 50:6a, where the prophet says: "I gave my back to those who struck me, and my cheeks [plural] to those who pulled out the beard." If Jesus had this particular passage of scripture in mind, then the purpose of the saying concerning the blow on both cheeks is that Jesus prophesied the fate of the prophets for his disciples.[20] But in that case, this saying must have been preceded by the mission charge, in which Jesus designated his disciples as being in the prophetic succession, and also by the prophecy that for him too the fate of suffering was appointed. The saying concerning the heresy-blow is not—let us say it once more—a matter of reaction to a general insult, but of outrage suffered as a consequence of following the suffering savior. If the disciples suffer the insulting blow because of their confession of Jesus, then they must accept it gladly as the taking up of a cross to follow him.[21]

Every word of the Sermon on the Mount was preceded by something else. The preaching of the kingdom of God preceded it. The granting of sonship to the disciples preceded it (Matt 5:16, 45, 48, and elsewhere). And Jesus' witness to himself in word and deed preceded it. The example of Jesus stands behind every word of the Sermon on the Mount. But this means the instructions of the Sermon have been torn out of their original context, although in many cases, as we have seen, this context has been preserved in parallel passages. All of them are, as it were, apodoses, which cannot be understood without the protasis, and which could not have been understood without the protasis at the time when Jesus spoke them.[22]

If I may express it with a touch of exaggeration, it is as if to every saying of the Sermon on the Mount we must supply the protasis: "Your sins are forgiven" (Matt 9:2). Therefore, because "Your sins are forgiven," there now follows: "While you are still in the way with your opponent, be reconciled to him quickly" (Matt 5:25). Because "Your sins are forgiven," there now follows: "If you do not forgive others their trespasses, neither can your Father forgive your trespasses" (Matt 6:15). Because "Your sins are forgiven," there now follows: "Love your enemies, and pray for those who persecute you" (Matt 5:44).

It might be better to say that the sayings of Jesus that have been brought together in the Sermon on the Mount are a part of the gospel. Each of these sayings reiterates that the old era is passing away. Through the proclamation of the gospel and through discipleship, you are transferred into the new era of God. And now you should know that this is what life is like when you belong to the new era of God. This is what sonship is like. This is what a lived faith is like. This is what the life of those who stand in the salvation-time of God is like, of those who are freed from the power of Satan and in whom the wonder of discipleship is consummated.

The fact that the Sermon on the Mount, ostensibly, retains only the apodoses and leaves out the protasis is not in itself surprising, when one remembers that in its present form it is an early Christian catechism. As such it is designed for a quite specific pedagogical purpose: it is intended to show the young Christians, who have not only heard the message of Jesus Christ but also opened their hearts to it, what manner of life they should lead in the future. In this case the protasis, if I may so express it, was given in the situation. The kerygma is now followed by the didache. Moreover, the protasis is only apparently missing. It is found at the beginning of the Sermon on the Mount in the form of the beatitudes (Matt 5:3-12) and in the sayings on the glory of discipleship (5:13-16). These two sections concern the whole Sermon, just as in a mathematical formula a number preceding the brackets concerns every entity within the brackets. They concern every saying in the Sermon on the Mount; they are simply not repeated every time.

Beginning with this recognition, which is absolutely decisive for a true understanding of the Sermon on the Mount, two further things are now understandable. First, the heavy nature of the demands that Jesus makes. His teaching on discipleship is directed to people for whom the power of Satan has already been destroyed by the Good News, to people who already stand in the kingdom of God and radiate its nature. It is spoken to people who have already received forgiveness, who have found the pearl of great price, who have been invited to the wedding, who through their faith in Jesus belong to the new creation, to the new world of God. It is directed to people who already know in their lives the great joy of which the parable of the hidden treasure speaks, in which the man joyfully goes and sells all that he has. It is directed to lost children, whom the father has already taken back into the home. To them Jesus says: You may live now in the time of salvation.

But the time of salvation is also the time when the will of God is valid in all its earnestness. The presence of the kingdom of God means establishment of the coming world's divine justice. This divine justice is at once sovereign forgiveness and the validity of God's holy will. Bestowal of divine forgiveness includes God's claim on the forgiven life. So speaks Jesus, and he does not hesitate to use the imperative, "You must." You should truly not be angry with your brother; you should truly avoid the impure look, strive for absolute truthfulness, and love your enemy. Only if we begin with the greatness of the gift of God can we really understand the heavy nature of the demands that Jesus makes.

Beginning with the recognition that something else preceded the Sermon on the Mount's teaching on discipleship we can go on to understand a second thing: the incompleteness of the Sermon on the Mount.[23] What Jesus teaches in the sayings collected in the Sermon on the Mount is not a complete regulation of the life of the disciples, and it is not intended to be. Rather, what is taught here are symptoms, signs, examples, of what it means when the kingdom of God breaks into the world, which is still under sin, death, and the devil. Jesus says in effect: I intend to show you, by means of some examples, what the new life is like, and what I show you through these examples you must apply to every aspect of life. You yourselves should be signs of the coming kingdom of God, signs that something has already happened. Through every aspect of your lives, including aspects beyond those of which I speak, you should testify to the world that the kingdom of God is already dawning. The victory of the kingdom of God should be visible in your lives, rooted and grounded in the kingdom of God.

"But who can accomplish this? We are poor-spirited, wavering people, driven to and fro." The disciples asked this question of Jesus. His answer to the objection is found in Matthew 5:14. This saying was uttered at a time when the disciples referred to their inability, their weakness. Then Jesus answered: "A city built on a hill cannot be hid." Gerhard von Rad has shown us, in a fine study, that this is not an ordinary city but the eschatological city of God.[24] Its light, says Jesus, shines in the world. You belong to it. In the eschatological city of God there is no need for convulsive efforts; its light shines of itself.

## Not Law, but Gospel

Thus the Sermon on the Mount is not law but gospel. For this is indeed the difference between law and gospel: The law leaves people to rely on their own strength and challenges them to do their utmost. The gospel, on the other hand, brings people before the gift of God and challenges them to make the inexpressible gift of God the basis for their lives. These are two different worlds. In order to make the difference clear, one should avoid the terms "Christian ethic," "Christian morality," and "Christian morals" in New Testament theology, because these secular expressions are inadequate and liable to misunderstanding. Instead of these, one should speak of "lived faith." Then it is clearly stated that the gift of God precedes God's demands.

If we take up once more the triad with which we began, we may now conclude. The sayings of Jesus that have been collected in the Sermon on the Mount are not intended to lay a legal yoke upon Jesus' disciples. They do not say: "You must do all of this in order that you may be saved (the perfectionist conception). Nor do they say: "You ought actually to have done all of this, seeing what poor creatures you are" (the theory of the impossible ideal). Nor in the sense: "Now pull yourself together; the final victory is at hand" (an interim-ethic). Rather, these sayings of Jesus delineate the lived faith. They say: You are forgiven; you are the child of God; you belong to God's kingdom. The sun of righteousness has risen over your life. You no longer belong to yourself; rather, you belong to the city of God, the light of which shines in the darkness. Now you may also experience it: out of the thankfulness of a redeemed child of God a new life is growing. That is the meaning of the Sermon on the Mount.

## NOTES

1. Hans Windisch, *The Meaning of the Sermon on the Mount*, trans. S. M. Gilmour (Philadelphia: Westminster, 1951; 2nd German ed., 1937).

2. *b. Šabb.* 31a, freely rendered. Compare C. G. Montefiore and H. Loewe, *A Rabbinic Anthology* (Philadelphia: Jewish Publication Society of America, 1960) 200 §539.

3. Windisch, *Meaning*, 71–72.

[4.] German: *Unerfüllbarkeitstheorie;* literally "theory of unfulfillabilty."

[5.] Johannes Weiss, *Jesus' Proclamation of the Kingdom of God*, trans. R. H. Hiers and D. L. Holland (Philadelphia: Fortress Press, 1971). *Die Predigt Jesu vom Reiche Gottes*. 2nd ed. Göttingen: Vandenhoeck and Ruprecht, 1900.

[6.] See, for example, Albert Schweitzer, *The Kingdom of God and Primitive Christianity*, ed. U. Neuenschwander, trans. L. A. Garrard (New York: Seabury, 1968; German ed. 1967); *The Mystery of the Kingdom of God: The Secret of Jesus' Messiahship and Passion*, trans. W. Lowrie (New York: Macmillan, 1950; German ed. 1901); *The Quest of the Historical Jesus*, 1st complete ed., trans. J. Bowden, FCBS (Minneapolis: Fortress Press, 2001; 2nd German ed. 1913).

[7.] Schweitzer, *Quest*, 315–54.

8. Weiss, *Predigt*, 150. (This passage is not in the English translation, which was based on the shorter first German edition.)

[9.] On other aspects of the structure of Matthew, see Ulrich Luz, *Matthew 1–7*, trans. W. Linss, CC (Minneapolis: Augsburg, 1989) 33–44; and K. C. Hanson, "Transformed on the Mountain: Ritual Analysis and the Gospel of Matthew," *Semeia* 67 (1994[95]) 147–70.

[10.] Jeremias was not an advocate of the Q (Sayings Source) hypothesis; but for a discussion of an Aramaic version of Q, see John S. Kloppenborg Verbin, *Excavating Q: The History and Setting of the Sayings Gospel* (Minneapolis: Fortress Press, 2000) 72–80; and James M. Robinson, "History of Q Research," in *The Critical Edition of Q*, ed. J. M. Robinson, P. Hoffman, J. S. Kloppenborg, Hermeneia Supplements (Minneapolis: Fortress Press, 2000), xxii–xxxiii. For other issues relating to Aramaic and the Gospels, see Matthew Black, *An Aramaic Approach to the Gospels and Acts* (Peabody, Mass.: Hendrickson, 1998); and Joseph A. Fitzmyer, "Methodology in the Study of the Aramaic Substratum of Jesus' Sayings in the New Testament," in *A Wandering Aramean: Collected Aramaic Essays*, SBLMS 25 (Missoula, Mont.: Scholars, 1979) 1–27.

[11.] For the composition of the Sermon on the Mount, see Hans Dieter Betz, *The Sermon on the Mount: A Commentary on the Sermon on the Mount, including the Sermon on the Plain (Matthew 5:3—7:27 and Luke 6:20-49)*, Hermeneia (Minneapolis: Fortress Press, 1995) 44–70.

12. C. H. Dodd, *The Apostolic Preaching and Its Development* (London: Hodder and Stoughton, 1936); idem, *Gospel and Law: The Relation of Faith and Ethics in Early Christianity* (New York: Columbia Univ. Press, 1951).

[13.] James I. H. McDonald, *Kerygma and Didache: The Articulation and Structure of the Earliest Christian Message*, SNTSMS 37 (Cambridge: Cambridge Univ. Press, 1980). For the nuances of kerygma and didache in Matthew, see Luz, *Matthew 1–7*, 206–8.

[14.] See Hans Dieter Betz, "A Jewish-Christian Cultic *Didache* in Matt. 6:1-18: Reflections and Questions on the Problem of the Historical Jesus," in *Essays on the Sermon on the Mount*, trans. L. L. Welborn (Philadelphia: Fortress Press, 1985) 55–69.

15. Literally "setting in life"; form critics employ this term to refer to those recurring religious and social situations in the life of the early Christian community that shaped the use of the Gospel materials.

[16.] On the scribes and Pharisees in the first century, see Joachim Jeremias, *Jerusalem in the Time of Jesus: An Investigation into Economic and Social Conditions during the New Testament Period*, trans. F. H. Cave and C. H. Cave (Philadelphia: Fortress Press, 1969) 233–67; Emil Schürer, *The History of the Jewish People in the Age of Jesus Christ*, rev. and ed. G. Vermes, F. Miller, M. Goodman (Edinburgh: T. & T. Clark, 1973–86) 2.322–25, 381–403; Anthony J. Saldarini, *Pharisees, Scribes and Sadducees in Palestinian Society: A Sociological Approach* (Wilmington, Del.: Glazier, 1988); Steve Mason, *Flavius Josephus on the Pharisees: A Composition-Critical Study*, StPB 39 (Leiden: Brill, 1991).

[17.] "Parenesis" (noun) and "parenetic" (adjective) are from the Greek *paraineō*, meaning "advise, counsel, instruct" and refer to ethical instruction. See James L. Bailey and Lyle D. Vander Broek, *Literary Forms in the New Testament* (Louisville: Westminster John Knox, 1992) 62–65; and Benjamin Fiore, "Parenesis and Protreptic," in *ABD* 5.162–65.

[18.] The interpretation of the beatitudes has been controversial. For recent approaches, see Betz, "The Beatitudes of the Sermon on the Mount (Matt. 5:3-12): Observations on Their Literary Form and Theological Significance," in

*Essays,* 17–36; Luz, *Matthew 1–7,* 224–46; Jerome H. Neyrey, "Loss of Wealth, Loss of Family and Loss of Honour: The Cultural Context of the Original Makarisms in Q," in *Modelling Early Christianity: Social-Scientific Studies of the New Testament in Its Context,* ed. P. F. Esler (London: Routledge, 1995) 139–58; and K. C. Hanson, "'How Honorable!' 'How Shameful!' A Cultural Analysis of Matthew's Makarisms and Reproaches," *Semeia* 68 (1994[96]) 81–111.

[19.] On the mission-sayings, see William E. Arnal, *Jesus and the Village Scribes: Galilean Conflicts and the Setting of Q* (Minneapolis: Fortress Press, 2001).

20. Karl Bornhäuser was the first to suggest that here Jesus may have been thinking of Isa 50:6; *Die Bergpredigt: Versuch einer zeitgenössischen Auslegung,* 2nd ed. BFCT 2/7 (Gütersloh: Bertelsmann, 1927) 113–15.

[21.] See Richard A. Horsley, *Jesus and the Spiral of Violence: Popular Jewish Resistance in Roman Palestine* (San Francisco: Harper and Row, 1987; reprint, Minneapolis: Fortress Press, 1993) 261–79. Horsley significantly cites *m. B. Qam.* 8.6, which refers to penalties for striking on the cheek, both forehand and backhand.

[22.] "Protasis" and "apodosis" are the grammatical designations for the two parts of a conditional sentence. The protasis is the clause expressing the condition (If x . . .); and the apodosis is the consequent clause (. . . then y).

[23.] Jeremias notes Herbert Girgensohn here but without a specific citation. He may have intended reference to *Teaching Luther's Catechism,* 2 vols., trans. J. W. Doberstein (Philadelphia: Muhlenberg, 1959–60).

24. Gerhard von Rad, "The City on the Hill," in *The Problem of the Hexateuch and Other Essays,* trans. E. W. T. Dicken (New York: McGraw-Hill, 1966) 232–42 (orig. German article, 1948–49).

# 3

# The Lord's Prayer

## THE LORD'S PRAYER IN THE ANCIENT CHURCH

During the time of Lent and Easter in the year 350 C.E., a Jerusalem pres-byter named Cyril, who was consecrated a bishop a year later, presented his celebrated twenty-four Catechetical Lectures in the Church of the Holy Sepulchre. These lectures, which have been preserved for us through the short-hand notes of one of Cyril's hearers, fall into two parts.[1] Those in the first part prepared the candidates for the baptism that they were to receive on Easter Eve. The focal point of these prebaptismal lectures was the exposition of the confession of faith, the Jerusalem Creed. The last five lectures, however, were presented during Easter week. These postbaptismal lectures instructed the newly baptized about the sacraments they had received. For this reason they were called "mystagogical catechetical lectures," that is, lectures that intro-duced the hearers to the "mysteries" or sacraments of the Christian faith. In the last of these mystagogical lectures, Cyril explains for his hearers the liturgy of the Mass, or Service of Holy Communion, especially the prayers that are spoken there. Among these is the Lord's Prayer.

This final (twenty-fourth) Catechetical Lecture by Cyril of Jerusalem is our earliest proof for the fact that the Lord's Prayer was regularly employed in the service. The position in the service where the Lord's Prayer was prayed is to be noted: it came immediately before the Communion. As a constituent part of the Communion liturgy, the Lord's Prayer belonged to that portion of the service in which only those who were baptized were permitted to participate, that is, it belonged to the so-called "Service for the Baptized" (*missa fidelium*). T. W. Manson has shown that this leads to the conclusion that knowledge of the Lord's Prayer and the privilege to use it were reserved for the full members of the church.[2]

What we have demonstrated for Jerusalem holds for the ancient church as a whole. Everywhere the Lord's Prayer was a constituent part of the celebration of the Lord's Supper; and everywhere the Lord's Prayer, together with the creed, belonged to those items in which the candidates for baptism were instructed either just before baptism or, as we saw in the case of Cyril, in the days directly after baptism. Petition by petition, the Lord's Prayer was explained, and then the whole prayer was repeated in an address to the converts. Thus those seeking baptism or those newly baptized learned the Lord's Prayer by heart. They were allowed to join in praying it for the first time in their first Service of Holy Communion, which was attached to the rite of their baptism. After this, they prayed it daily, and it formed a token of their identification as Christians. Because the privilege of praying the Lord's Prayer was limited to the baptized members of the church, it was called the "prayer of believers."

The connection of the Lord's Prayer with baptism can be traced back to early times. In the beginning of the second century, we find a variant to Luke 11:2 that reads: "Your Holy Spirit come upon us and cleanse us." The heretic Marcion had this instead of the first petition. His wording of the Lord's Prayer seems to have been as follows:

> Father,
>     your Holy Spirit come upon us and cleanse us.
> Your kingdom come.
> Your bread for the morrow give us day by day.
> And forgive us our sins,
>     for we also forgive everyone who is indebted to us.
> And do not allow us to be led into temptation.

Two of the Greek minuscule manuscripts (numbers 162 and 700) and two late church fathers (Gregory of Nyssa [c. 330–395] and Maximus the Confessor [c. 580–662]) have the petition for the Holy Spirit instead of the second petition. It is quite improbable that the petition for the Holy Spirit should be the original text; its attestation is much too weak. From where, then, does this petition originate? We know that it was an old baptismal prayer, and we may conclude that it was added to the Lord's Prayer when this was used at the baptismal rite. One may compare the fact that the Marcionite version of the Prayer, quoted above, has "your bread" in the petition for bread. This is probably an allusion to the Lord's Supper; thus Marcion has both sacraments in view, baptism in this first petition and the Lord's Supper, which followed baptism, in his phrase "your bread."

But we must go even one step further back. The connection of the Lord's Prayer with baptism that we have found already in the first part of the second century can be traced back even into the first century. It is true that at first glance we seem to get a completely different picture when we turn to the *Didache* (or *Teaching of the Twelve Apostles*). This document is the oldest "church order," the basic part of which is dated by recent commentator, perhaps somewhat too optimistically, as early as 50–70 C.E.,[3] but which in all likelihood does nonetheless belong in the first Christian century. In *Didache* 8:2 the Lord's Prayer is cited, word for word, introduced by the admonition, "And do not pray as the wicked [do]; pray instead this way, as the Lord directed in his gospel." The Prayer concludes with a doxology consisting of two terms, "For power and glory are yours forever." In 8:3 there then follows the advice: "Pray this way three times daily." Here, in the earliest period, regular use of the Lord's Prayer is therefore presupposed, though without any apparent connection with the sacraments. Yet the impression is false. The matter becomes clear if one notes the context in which the Lord's Prayer stands in the *Didache*.[4] The *Didache* begins with the instruction in the "Two Ways," the Way of Life and the Way of Death (chaps. 1–6). This teaching no doubt belonged to the instruction of candidates for baptism. Chapter 7 treats baptism; then begin the sections that are important for those who are baptized: fasting and prayer (including the Lord's Prayer) are treated in chapter 8, the Lord's Supper in chapters 9–10, and church organization and church discipline in chapters 11–15. For us it is important to note that the Lord's Prayer and the Lord's Supper follow upon baptism. This corroborates the point we made at the beginning: the Lord's Prayer was intended in the early church—beginning already in the first century, as we can now add—only for those who were full members of the church.

All this leads to a very important result, which Manson again has pointed out most lucidly.[5] While today the Lord's Prayer is understood as common property of all people, it was not so in earliest times. As one of the most holy treasures of the church, the Lord's Prayer, together with the Lord's Supper, was reserved for full members, and it was not disclosed to those who stood outside. It was a privilege to be allowed to pray it. The great reverence and awe that surrounded it is best seen by the introductory formulas found both in the liturgies of the East and in those of the West. In the East, in the so-called Liturgy of St. John Chrysostom, which even today is still the usual form of the mass among the Greek and Russian Orthodox churches, the priest prays at the introduction of the Lord's Prayer, "And make us worthy, O Lord, that we joyously and without presumption may make bold to invoke you, the heavenly God, as Father, and to say: Our Father." The formula in the Roman Mass is similar: "We make bold to say (*audemus dicere*): Our Father."

This awesome reverence given the Lord's Prayer was a reality in the ancient church, which unfortunately has been lost to us today for the most part. That should make us uneasy. We ought to ask ourselves, therefore, whether we can again discover why the early church surrounded the Lord's Prayer with such reverence, so that they said, "We make bold to say, Our Father." Perhaps we may regain an inkling of the basis for this awe if, with the aid of the results from recent New Testament research, we try to discover as best we can how Jesus himself meant the words of the Lord's Prayer.

## THE EARLIEST TEXT OF THE LORD'S PRAYER

We must first clear up a preliminary question, namely that of the earliest text of the Lord's Prayer. The Lord's Prayer has been handed down to us at two places in the New Testament: in Matthew as part of the Sermon on the Mount (Matt 6:9-13) and in Luke 11:2-4. Before trying to consider the original meaning of the petitions of the Prayer, we must face the strange fact that the two evangelists, Matthew and Luke, transmit it in slightly different wordings. It is true that in the King James Version the differences are limited, the main divergence being that in Luke the doxology is absent—that is, "For yours is the kingdom, the power, and the glory, forever." Likewise, in the many editions of the Luther Bible in German, the two versions agree with one another, save for trivial variations and the absence of the doxology in Luke. But as a matter of fact, the divergences are greater than this. In the Revised Standard Version or in the New English Bible translations, just as in the *Zürcherbibel* (but not in the latest edition of the Luther Bible), we read a form of the Lord's Prayer in Luke 11:2-4 that is briefer than that found in Matthew.[6]

It is well known that in the last one hundred and twenty years research into the oldest text-form of the New Testament has gone forward with great energy, first in Germany, and then in England, and in the last decades also in America, and admirable results have been achieved in recovering the oldest text. This work was triggered by the discovery of numerous manuscripts of the New Testament, often very ancient ones. In 1963 the number of New Testament manuscripts in Greek alone totaled 4,903.[7] By comparing and classifying these manuscripts, scholars have succeeded in working out an earlier text than that which the King James translators or Luther possessed. While for the translators in 1611 or for Luther the text-form was available much as it had been developed at the end of the fourth century in the Byzantine church, today we know the text of approximately the second century. One can say, without exaggeration, that this chapter in research is essentially concluded and that we today have attained the best possible Greek text of the New Testament. With regard to the Lord's Prayer, the results are as follows: At the time when the Gospels of Matthew and Luke were being composed (c. 75–85 C.E.), the Lord's Prayer was being transmitted in two forms that agreed with each other in essentials, but which differed in the fact that the one was longer than the other. The longer form appears in Matthew 6:9-13, and also, with insignificant variants, in the *Didache* 8:2. The briefer form appears in Luke 11:2-4.

While the Matthean version agrees with that form that is familiar to us, a form of the Prayer with seven petitions (only the doxology is missing in Matthew), the Lukan version has only five petitions according to the oldest manuscripts. It runs:

> Father,
> Hallowed be your name.
> Your kingdom come.
> Give us each day our bread for tomorrow.
> And forgive us our sins,
> for we also forgive everyone who is indebted to us.
> And let us not succumb to the trial.

Two questions now arise. How is it that about the year 75 c.e. the Lord's Prayer was being transmitted and prayed in two forms that diverged from one another? And which of the two forms is to be regarded as the original?

## The Two Forms

The answer to the first question concerning the two forms emerges when we observe the context in which the Lord's Prayer occurs in Matthew and Luke. In both cases the Lord's Prayer occurs with words of Jesus that treat prayer.

In Matthew we read, in the section 6:1-18, a discussion that opposes the type of piety practiced in the lay circles that formed the Pharisaic movement. The Lord reproves the fact that they offer their alms (6:2-4) and their prayers (6:5-6) and conduct their fasts (6:16-18) publicly for show and thus use them to serve their craving for approval and to feed their own self-conceit. In contrast he demands of his disciples that their almsgiving and prayer and fasting shall take place in secret, so that only God beholds it. The three units are symmetrically constructed: in each instance false and right conduct are contrasted with each other through two *when* clauses. But the middle unit, which deals with prayer (6:5-6), is expanded through three further words of Jesus about prayer, so that the following structure arose.

1. The foundation was provided by the admonition of Jesus that his disciples were not to be like the Pharisees who arrange things so that they find themselves in the midst of the tumult of the marketplace when trumpet blasts from the temple announce the hour of prayer. This results—evidently to their complete surprise—in their having to pray among the throng of people.

No, Jesus' disciples are to pray behind closed doors, even, if need be, in so worldly a place as the storeroom (Greek *tamieion;* RSV "your room"; 6:5-6).

2. Joined to this is Jesus' admonition not to "heap up empty phrases as the Gentiles do." As children of the heavenly Father, his disciples do not need to employ "many words" (6:7-8).

3. The Lord's Prayer follows as an example of brief prayer (6:9-13). As a matter of fact, this prayer from the Lord is distinguished from most prayers in late Judaism by its brevity.

4. Emphatic in its position at the end of this middle section is a saying of Jesus about inner disposition in prayer, a saying that connects with the petition on forgiveness: only the one who is ready to forgive has the right to petition God for forgiveness (6:14-15).

We thus have before us in Matthew 6:5-15 a catechism on prayer put together from words of Jesus, a catechism that would be employed in the instruction of the newly baptized.

Also in Luke, the Lord's Prayer occurs in such a catechism on prayer (Luke 11:1-13). This indicates how important the earliest church considered the instruction of its members in the right kind of prayer. In Luke, however, the catechism on prayer is of a very different sort from that found in Matthew. But it also falls into four parts.

1. A picture of the Lord at prayer as a prototype for all Christian prayer is prefixed, as well as the request of the disciples, "Lord, teach us to pray" (11:1).

2. The parable about the man who knocks on his friend's door at midnight is added here. In its present context it presents an admonition to persist in prayer, even if one's prayer is not heard immediately (11:5-8).

3. The same admonition then follows in imperative form: "Ask, and it shall be given to you" (11:9-10).

4. The conclusion is formed by the picture of the father who "gives good gifts" to his children (11:11-13).

The differences in these two primers on prayer are to be explained by the fact that they are directed at very different groups of people. The Matthean catechism on prayer is addressed to people who have learned to pray in childhood but whose prayer stands in danger of becoming a routine. The Lukan catechism on prayer, on the other hand, is addressed to people who must learn to pray for the first time and whose courage to pray must be aroused. It is clear that Matthew is transmitting to us instruction on prayer directed at Jewish Christians, Luke at Gentile Christians. About 75 C.E., therefore, the Lord's Prayer was a fixed element in instructions on prayer in all Christian circles, in the Jewish-Christian as well as in the Gentile-Christian church. Both churches, different as their situations were, were at one on this point: that a Christian learned to pray from the Lord's Prayer.

For our question then (concerning why the two forms in Matthew and Luke vary from each other), the conclusion is that the variations can in no case be traced back to the caprice of the evangelists—no author would have dared to make such alteration in the Prayer on his own. Rather, the variations are to be seen within a broader context: we have before us the wording for the Prayer from two churches, that is, different liturgical wordings of the Lord's Prayer. Each of the evangelists transmits to us the wording of the Lord's Prayer as it was prayed in his church at that time.

## The Original Form

Now we can deal with the second question: Which of the two forms is to be regarded as the original?

If we compare the two texts carefully, the most striking divergence is the difference in length. The Lukan form is shorter than that of Matthew at three places. First, the invocation is shorter. Luke says only "Father," or properly "Dear Father," in Greek *pater*, in Aramaic *'abba'*, whereas Matthew says, according to the pious and reverent form of Palestinian invocation, "Our Father who art in heaven." Second, whereas Matthew and Luke agree in the first two petitions—the "Thou-petitions" ("Hallowed be your name" and "Your kingdom come")—there follows in Matthew a third "Thou-petition": "Your will be done in earth, as it is in heaven." Third, in Matthew the last of the following "We-petitions" has an antithesis. Luke has only "And let us not suc-cumb to the trial"; but Matthew adds "but deliver us from evil."

Now if we ask which form is the original—the longer form of Matthew or the shorter form of Luke—the decisive observation, which has not yet been mentioned, is the following: the shorter form of Luke is completely contained in the longer form of Matthew. This makes it very probable that the Matthean form is an expanded one. According to all that we know about the tendency of liturgical texts to conform to certain laws in their transmission, in a case where the shorter version is contained in the longer one, the shorter text is to be regarded as original. No one would have dared to shorten a sacred text like the Lord's Prayer and leave out two petitions if they had formed part of the original tradition. On the contrary, the reverse is amply attested, that in the early period, before wordings were fixed, liturgical texts were elaborated, expanded, and enriched.

This conclusion, that the Matthean version represents an expansion, is confirmed by three supplementary observations. First, the three expansions that we find in Matthew, as compared with Luke, are always found toward the end of a section of the prayer: the first at the end of the address, the sec-ond at the end of the "Thou-petitions," and the third at the end of the "We-petitions." This again is exactly in accordance with what we find elsewhere in the growth of liturgical texts; they show a tendency for grand expansions at the end.

Second, it is of further significance that in Matthew the stylistic structure is more consistently carried through. Three "Thou-petitions" in Matthew correspond to the three "We-petitions" (the sixth and seventh petitions in Matthew were regarded as one petition). The third "We-petition," which in Luke seems abrupt because of its brevity, is assimilated in Matthew to the first two "We-petitions." To spell this out, the first two "We-petitions" show a parallelism:

> Our bread for tomorrow / give us today.
> Forgive us / as we forgive.

In Luke, however, the third "We-petition" is shorter, apparently intentionally:

> And let us not succumb to the trial.

But Matthew offers a parallelism here too:

> And lead us not into temptation / but deliver us from evil.

This endeavor to produce parallelism in lines (*parallelismus membrorum*) is a characteristic of liturgical tradition. One can see the point especially well if one compares the various versions of the words of institution at the Lord's Supper.[8]

Third, a final point in favor of the originality of the Lukan version is the reappearance of the brief form of address "dear Father" (*'abba'*) in the prayers of the earliest Christians, as we see from Romans 8:15 and Galatians 4:6. Matthew has a grand address, "Our Father who is in the heavens," such as corresponded to pious Jewish-Palestinian custom. We shall see that the simple *'abba'* was a unique note in Jesus' own prayers. Thus we must conclude that this plain *'abba'* was the original address.[9]

All these observations lead us, then, in the same direction. The common substance of both texts, which is identical with its Lukan form, is the oldest text. The Gentile-Christian church has handed down the Lord's Prayer without change, whereas the Jewish-Christian church, which lived in a world of rich liturgical tradition and used a variety of prayer forms, has enriched the Lord's Prayer liturgically.[10] Because the form transmitted by Matthew was the more richly elaborated one, it soon permeated the whole church; we saw above that the *Didache* presents this form as well.

Of course, we must be cautious with our conclusions. The possibility remains that Jesus himself spoke the "Our Father" on different occasions in a slightly differing form, a shorter one and a longer one. But perhaps it would be safer to say that the shorter Lukan form is in all probability the oldest one, whereas Matthew gives us the earliest evidence that the Lord's Prayer was used liturgically in worship. In any case, the chief thing is that both texts agree in the decisive elements.

Nonetheless, the question about the original form of the Lord's Prayer is still not completely answered. We have thus far directed our attention only to the varying lengths of the two versions. But in the lines where they share a common wording, these versions also exhibit certain (admittedly not very significant) variations, specifically in the second part, the "We-petitions." To these differences we now turn briefly.

The first "We-petition" for daily bread reads in Matthew, "Give us this day our bread for tomorrow." As we shall see later, the contrast of "this day" and "for tomorrow" sets the whole tone for the verse. In Luke, on the other hand, it reads, "Give us each day our bread for tomorrow." Here the term "this day" is expanded into "each day"; the petition is thereby broadened into a generalized saying, with the consequence that the antithesis "this day—for tomorrow" drops out. Moreover, in Luke the Greek word for "give" now had to be expressed with the present imperative (*didou*, literally "keep on giving!"), whereas elsewhere throughout the Prayer the aorist imperative is used, which denotes a single action. Matthew also has the aorist imperative in this petition (*dos*, "give!"). From all this it may be concluded that the Matthean form of the petition for daily bread is the older one.

In the second "We-petition" (for forgiveness), Matthew has "Forgive us our debts," while Luke has "Forgive us our sins." Now it was a peculiarity of Jesus' mother tongue, Aramaic, that the word *ḥobha* was used for "sin," though it properly meant a debt, "money owed." Matthew translates the word quite literally with "debts" (Greek *opheilēmata*, a word that is not common in Greek for "sin." This enables one to see that the Lord's Prayer goes back to an Aramaic wording. In the Lukan version, the word "debts" is represented by the usual Greek word for "sins" (*hamartiai*); but the wording in the next clause makes it evident that in the initial clause "debts" had originally appeared: "for we ourselves forgive everyone who is *indebted* to us." In this case, too, Matthew therefore has the older wording.

The same picture results when one focuses attention on yet a final variation in wording. We read in Matthew (literally translated): "as we also have forgiven (*aphēkamen*) our debtors." In Luke, on the other hand, we read: "for we also ourselves forgive (*aphiomen*) everyone who is indebted to us." When we ask which formulation is the older, the past tense in Matthew or the present tense form in Luke, it is readily seen that Matthew has the more difficult form, and in such cases the more difficult form is to be regarded as the more original. Matthew's is the more difficult form, because his wording ("as we have forgiven") could lead to the mistaken impression that our forgiving must not only precede forgiveness on God's part, but also that it provides the standard for God's forgiving us: "forgive us thus, as we have forgiven." In actuality, however, behind Matthew's past tense form lies what is called in Semitic grammar a "present perfect," which refers to an action occurring here and now. The correct translation of the Matthean form would therefore run "as we also with this forgive our debtors." By its choice of the present tense form, Luke's version was intended to exclude a misunderstanding among Greek-speaking Christians, since it says (and this catches the sense): "for we also ourselves forgive everyone who is indebted to us." Moreover, in the Lukan form, the petition on forgiveness is broadened by the addition of the word "everyone," which represents a sharpening of the meaning in that it permits no exceptions in our forgiving.

Comparison of the wording of the two forms of the Lord's Prayer therefore shows that the Lukan form has been assimilated at several points to Greek linguistic usage, when compared to Matthew. Viewed as a whole, our results may be summarized thus: the Lukan version has preserved the oldest form with respect to *length*, but the Matthean text is more original with regard to *wording*.

In our consideration of the petition for forgiveness, we have just observed that the Matthean phrase "our debts" enables one to see that the Lord's Prayer, which is of course preserved for us only in Greek, goes back to an original Aramaic version. As we shall see below, this observation is confirmed by the fact that the two "Thou-petitions" relate to an Aramaic prayer, the *Qaddiš*. When one attempts to put the Lord's Prayer back into Aramaic, Jesus' mother tongue, the conclusion begins to emerge that, like the Old Testament Psalter, Jesus' prayer is couched in liturgical language. Even the person who brings no knowledge of the Semitic languages to the following attempt at retranslation can easily spot the characteristic features of this solemn language. We should note three features especially: parallelism, the two-beat rhythm, and the rhyme in lines two and four, which is scarcely accidental. The Lord's Prayer in Jesus' tongue sounded something like this, with the accents designating the two-beat rhythm:[11]

> *'Abba'*
> *yithaqaddáš šemákh / tethé malkhuthákh*
> *laḥmán delimḥár / habh lán yoma' dhén*
> *ushebhoq lán ḥobhain / kedhiš bháqnan leḥayyabhaín*
> *wela' tha'elínnan lenisyón.*

## THE MEANING OF THE LORD'S PRAYER

Having considered what can be said about the original wording, we are prepared to face the main question: What was, as far as we can judge, the original meaning?

Luke reports that Jesus gave the Lord's Prayer to his disciples on a quite specific occasion. "He was praying in a certain place, and when he ceased, one of his disciples said to him, 'Lord, teach us to pray, as John taught his disciples'" (Luke 11:1). That the unnamed disciple appealed to the example of John the Baptist is important for our understanding of the Lord's Prayer, since we know that at the time of Jesus individual religious groups were marked by their own prayer customs and forms. This was true of the Pharisees, the Essenes, and, as we perceive from Luke 11:1, the disciples of John as well. A particular custom in prayer expressed the particular relationship with God that bound the individuals together. The request at Luke 11:1, therefore, shows that Jesus' disciples recognized themselves as a community, namely, as the community of the age of salvation. Furthermore, they requested of Jesus a prayer that would bind them together and identify them, by bringing to expression their chief concern. As a matter of fact, the Lord's Prayer is the clearest and, in spite of its terseness, the richest summary of Jesus' proclamation that we possess. When the Lord's Prayer was given to the disciples, prayer in Jesus' name began (John 14:13-14; 15:16; 16:23).[12]

The structure of the Lord's Prayer is simple and transparent. We present once again what is presumably the old wording, which follows the short form according to Luke (with minor variations of wording that follows Matthew):

> Dear Father,
> hallowed be your name.
> Your kingdom come,
> our bread for tomorrow, give us today.
> And forgive us our debts,
> as we also herewith forgive our debtors.
> And let us not succumb to the trial.

The structure of the Lord's Prayer then consists of:

1. The address
2. Two "Thou-petitions" in parallel (three in Matthew)
3. Two "We-petitions" in parallel, both forming an antithesis, as we shall see
4. The concluding request

We also observe what seems to be an apparently insignificant point: while the two "Thou-petitions" stand side by side without any "and," the two parallel "We-petitions" are connected by an "and."

## The Address "Dear Father" ('Abba')

When we trace back to its earliest beginnings the history of the invocation of God as Father, we have the feeling of descending into a mine in which new and unexpected treasures are disclosed one after another. It is surprising to see that already in the ancient Near East, as early as the third and second millennia B.C.E., we find the deity addressed as father. We find this title for the first time in Sumerian prayers, long before the time of Moses and the prophets, and there already the word "father" does not merely refer to the deity as pro-creator and ancestor of the king and of the people and as powerful lord, but it also has quite another significance: it is used for the "merciful, gracious father, in whose hand the life of the whole land lies" in a hymn from Ur to the moon god Sin.[13] For those in the ancient Near East, the word "father," as applied to God, thus encompasses, from earliest times, something of what the word "mother" signifies among us.

When we turn to the Old Testament, we find that God is only seldom spo-ken of as Father—in fact, only on fourteen occasions, but all these are impor-tant. God is Israel's Father, but now not mythologically as procreator or ancestor, but as the one who elected, delivered, and saved his people Israel by mighty deeds in history. This designation of God as Father in the Old Testa-ment comes to full fruition, however, in the message of the prophets. God is Israel's Father. But the prophets must make constant accusation against God's people that Israel has not given God the honor that a son should give to his father.

> A son honors his father,
>     and a servant his master.
> If then I am a father,
>     where is my honor?
> And if I am a master,
>     where is my fear?
>     says Yahweh of Hosts to you.
>                 (Mal 1:6; see Deut 32:5-6; Jer 3:19-20)

And Israel's answer to this rebuke is a confession of sin and the reiterated cry, "You are our father" (*'abhinu 'atta;* Isa 63:15-16; 64:7-8; Jer 3:4). And God's reply to this cry is mercy beyond all understanding:

Is Ephraim my dear son?
   Is he the child I delight in?
As often as I speak against him,
   I still remember him.
Therefore I am deeply moved for him;
   I will surely have mercy on him,
     says Yahweh. (Jer 31:20)

Can there be any deeper dimension to the term "father" than this compulsive, forgiving mercy that is beyond comprehension?

When we turn to Jesus' preaching, the answer must be: Yes, here there is something quite new, absolutely new—the word *'abba'*. From the prayer in Gethsemane (Mark 14:36) we learn that Jesus addressed God with this word, and this point is confirmed not only by Romans 8:15 and Galatians 4:6, but also by the striking oscillation of the forms for the vocative "O father" in the Greek text of the Gospels, an oscillation that is to be explained only through the fact that the Aramaic term *'abba'* lies behind all such passages.[14]

With the help of my assistants, I have examined the prayer literature of late Judaism—a large, rich literature all too infrequently explored. The result of this examination was that in no place in this immense literature is this invocation of God as *'abba'* to be found. How is this to be explained? The church fathers John Chrysostom, Theodor of Mopsuestia, and Theodoret of Cyrrhus—who originated from Antioch where the populace spoke the West Syrian dialect of Aramaic, and who probably had Aramaic-speaking nurses—testify unanimously that *'abba'* was the address of the small child to his father. And the Talmud confirms this when it says: "When a child experiences the taste of wheat [that is, when it is weaned], it learns to say *'abba'* ['dear father'] and *'imma'* ['dear mother']" (*b. Ber.* 40; *b. Sanh.* 70b).

*'Abba'* and *'imma'* are thus the first sounds that the child stammers. But these terms were not limited to small children; grown sons and daughters also used them to address their parents. *'Abba'* was an everyday word, a homey family word, a secular word, the tender, filial address to a father: "Dear father." No Jew would have dared to address God in this manner. Jesus did it always, in all his prayers that are handed down to us, with one single exception, the cry from the cross: "My God, my God, why have you forsaken me?" (Mark 15:34; Matt 27:46). Here the term of address for God was prescribed by the fact that Jesus was quoting Psalm 22:1.

Jesus thus spoke with God as a son would with his father: simply, intimately, securely, filial in manner. But his invocation of God as *'abba'* is not to be understood merely psychologically, as a step toward growing apprehension of God. Rather, we learn from Matthew 11:27 that Jesus himself viewed this filial form of address for God as the heart of that revelation that had been granted him by the Father. In this term *'abba'* the ultimate mystery of his mission and his authority is expressed. He, to whom the Father had granted full knowledge of God, had the messianic prerogative of addressing him with the familiar address of a son. This term *'abba'* is an *ipsissima vox* of Jesus and contains in principle his message and his claim to have been sent from the Father.[15]

The final point, and the most astonishing of all, however, has yet to be mentioned: in the Lord's Prayer Jesus authorizes his disciples to repeat the word *'abba'* after him. He gives them a share in his sonship and empowers them, as his disciples, to speak with their heavenly Father in just such a familiar, trusting way as a child would with his father. Yes, he goes so far as to say that it is this new childlike relationship that first opens the doors to God's reign: "Truly, I say to you, unless you become like children again you will not find entrance into the kingdom of God" (Matt 18:3).[16] Children can say *'abba'!* Only he who, through Jesus, lets himself be given the childlike trust that resides in the word *'abba'* finds his way into the kingdom of God. The apostle Paul also understood this; he says twice that there is no surer sign or guarantee of the possession of the Holy Spirit and of the gift of sonship than this, that one is bold to repeat this one word, "*Abba*, dear Father" (Rom 8:15; Gal 4:6). Perhaps at this point we get some inkling why the use of the Lord's Prayer was not commonplace in the early church and why it was spoken with such reverence and awe: "Make us worthy, O Lord, that we joyously and without presumption may make bold to invoke you, the heavenly God, as Father, and to say, Our Father."

### The Two "Thou-Petitions"

The first words that the child says to his heavenly Father are, "Hallowed be your name, your kingdom come." These two petitions are not only parallel in structure, but they also correspond to one another in content. They recall the *Qaddiš* ("Holy"), an ancient Aramaic prayer that formed the conclusion of the service in the synagogue and with which Jesus was no doubt familiar from childhood. What is probably the oldest form of this prayer (later expanded) runs:

> Exalted and hallowed be his great name
>     in the world that he created according to his will.
> May he rule his kingdom
>     in your lifetime and in your days
>     and in the lifetime of the whole house of Israel,
>       speedily and soon.
> And to this, say "Amen."

It is from this connection with the *Qaddiš* that we can explain the way in which the two "Thou-petitions" (in contrast to the two parallel "We-petitions") stand alongside each other without any connecting word; for in the earliest texts of the *Qaddiš* the two petitions about the hallowing of the name and the coming of the kingdom appear not to be connected by an "and."

Comparison with the *Qaddiš* also shows that the two petitions are eschatological. They make entreaty for the revelation of God's eschatological kingdom. Every accession to power by an earthly ruler is accompanied by homage in words and gestures. So it will be when God enters upon his rule. Then people will do homage to him, hallowing his name: "Holy, holy, holy, the Lord God the Almighty, who was and is and is to come" (Rev 4:8). Then they will all prostrate themselves at the feet of the King of kings, saying, "We give thanks to you, Lord God Almighty, who are and who were, for you have taken your great power and begun to reign" (Rev 11:17). The two "Thou-petitions"—to which Matthew adds yet a third one of like meaning ("Your will be done, on earth as it is in heaven")—thus make entreaty for the final consummation. Their contents strike the same note as the prayer of the early church, *Maranatha* (1 Cor 16:22), "Come, Lord Jesus" (Rev 22:20). They seek the hour in which God's profaned and misused name will be glorified and his reign revealed, in accordance with the promise, "I will sanctify my great name, which has been profaned among the nations, and which you have profaned among them; and the nations shall know that I am Yahweh, says the Lord Yahweh, when through you I display my holiness before their eyes" (Ezek 36:23).

These petitions are a cry out of the depths of distress. Out of a world that is enslaved under the rule of evil and in which Christ and Antichrist are locked in conflict, Jesus' disciples, seemingly a prey of evil and death and Satan, lift their eyes to the Father and cry out for the revelation of God's glory. But at the same time, these petitions are an expression of absolute certainty. Those who pray this way take seriously God's promise, in spite of all the demonic powers, and put themselves completely in God's hands, with imperturbable trust: "You will complete your glorious work, *'abba'*, Father."

These are the same words that the Jewish community prays in the synagogue at the end of the service in the *Qaddiš*. Yet the two "Thou-petitions" are not the same as the *Qaddiš*, in spite of the similar wording. There is a great difference. In the *Qaddiš* the prayer is by a congregation that stands in the darkness of the present age and asks for the consummation.[17] In the Lord's Prayer, though similar words are used, a congregation is praying that knows that the turning point has already come, because God has already begun his saving work. This congregation now makes supplication for full revelation of what has already been granted.

### The Two "We-Petitions"

The two "We-petitions" for daily bread and for forgiveness hang together as closely as the two "Thou-petitions." This connection of the two "We-petitions" with one another is seen immediately in the structure through the fact that both of them, in contrast to the "Thou-petitions," consist of *two* half-lines each:

> Our bread for tomorrow / give us today.
> And forgive us our debts / as we forgive our debtors.

If it is correct that the two "Thou-petitions" recall the *Qaddiš*, then we must conclude that in the Lord's Prayer the accent lies completely on the new material that Jesus added, that is, the two "We-petitions." They form the real heart of the Lord's Prayer, to which the two "Thou-petitions" lead up.

*Bread.* The first of the two "We-petitions" asks for daily bread (Greek *artos epiousios*). The Greek word *epiousios*, which Martin Luther rendered *täglich* ("daily") and William Tyndale in 1525 and the King James Version rendered as "daily," has been the object of lengthy discussion that is not yet finally settled. In my opinion, the decisive fact is that the church father Jerome (c. 342–420) tells us that in the lost Aramaic *Gospel of the Nazarenes* the term *mahar* appears, meaning "tomorrow"; here, therefore, the reference was to bread "for tomorrow." Now it is true that this *Gospel of the Nazarenes* is not older than our first three Gospels; rather, it rests on our Gospel of Matthew.[18] Nonetheless, the Aramaic wording of the Lord's Prayer in the *Gospel of the Nazarenes* ("bread for tomorrow") must be older than the *Gospel of the Nazarenes* itself and older even than our Gospels. For in first-century Palestine the Lord's Prayer was prayed in uninterrupted usage in Aramaic, and someone translating the Gospel of Matthew into Aramaic naturally did not translate the Lord's Prayer as he did the rest of the text. Instead, when the translator came to Matthew 6:9-13, he of course stopped translating; he simply wrote down the holy words in the form in which he prayed them day by day. In other words, the Aramaic-speaking Jewish-Christians, among whom the Lord's Prayer lived on in its original Aramaic wording in unbroken usage since the days of Jesus, prayed, "Our bread for tomorrow give us today."

Jerome tells us even more. He adds a remark telling how the phrase "bread for tomorrow" was understood. He says, "In the so-called *Gospel according to the Hebrews* . . . I found *mahar,* which means 'for tomorrow,' so that the sense is, 'Our bread for tomorrow—that is, our future bread—give us today.'[19] As a matter of fact, in late Judaism *mahar,* meant not only the next day, but also the great Tomorrow, the final consummation. Accordingly, Jerome is saying, the "bread for tomorrow" was not meant as earthly bread but as the bread of life. Further, we know from the ancient translations of the Lord's Prayer, both in the East and in the West, that in the early church this eschatological under-standing—"bread of the age of salvation," "bread of life," "heavenly manna"—was the familiar, if not the predominant interpretation of the phrase "bread for tomorrow."

Since primeval times, the bread of life and the water of life have been sym-bols of paradise, an epitome of the fullness of all God's material and spiritual gifts. It is this bread—symbol, image, and fulfillment of the age of salvation—to which Jesus is referring when he says that in the consummation he will eat and drink with his disciples (Luke 22:30). And he will gird himself and serve them at table (Luke 12:37) with the bread that has been broken and the cup that has been blessed (see Matt 26:29). The eschatological thrust of all the other petitions in the Lord's Prayer speaks for the fact that the petition for bread has an eschatological sense too; that is, it entreats God for the bread of life.

This interpretation may perhaps be a surprise or even a disappointment for us. For so many people it is important that at least *one* petition in the Lord's Prayer should lead into everyday life, the petition for daily bread. Is that to be taken away from us? Is that not an impoverishment? No, in reality, appli-cation of the petition about bread to the bread of life is a great enrichment. It would be a gross misunderstanding if one were to suppose that here there is a "spiritualizing," after the manner of Greek philosophy, and that there is a dis-tinction made between "earthly" and "heavenly" bread. For Jesus, earthly bread and the bread of life are not antithetical. In the realm of God's kingship, he viewed all earthly things as hallowed. His disciples belong to God's new age; they are snatched away from the age of death (Matt 8:22). This fact mani-fests itself in their life down to the last details. It expresses itself in their words (Matt 5:21-22, 33-37), in their looks (5:28), in the way they greet people on the street (5:47); it expresses itself also in their eating and drinking. For the disci-ples of Jesus there are no longer "clean" and "unclean" foods. "There is noth-ing outside a person that by going in can defile" (Mark 7:15a); all that God provides is blessed.

This hallowing of life is most clearly illustrated by the picture of Jesus at table for a meal. The bread that he offered when he sat at table with publicans and sinners was everyday bread, and yet it was more: it was bread of life. The bread that he broke for his disciples at the Last Supper was earthly bread, and yet it was more: his body given for many in death, the gift of a portion in the atoning power of his death. Every meal his disciples had with him involved the usual eating and drinking, and yet it was more: a meal of salvation, a mes-sianic meal, image and anticipation of the meal at the consummation, because he was the master of the house. This remained true in the earliest churches: their daily fellowship meals were the customary meals for suste-nance, and yet at the same time they were a "Lord's supper" (1 Cor 11:20) that mediated fellowship with him and linked in fellowship with one another those sitting at table (1 Cor 10:16-17). In the same way, for all his followers, every meal is a meal in his presence. He is the host who fills the hungry and thirsty with the fullness of his blessings.

It is in this sense too that the petition about "bread for tomorrow" is intended. It does not sever everyday life and the kingdom of God from one another, but it encompasses the totality of life. It embraces everything that Jesus' disciples need for body and soul. It includes "daily bread," but it does not content itself with that. It asks that amid the secularity of everyday life the powers and gifts of God's coming age might be active in all that Jesus' disciples do in word and deed. One can flatly say that this petition for the bread of life makes entreaty for the hallowing of everyday life.

Only when one has perceived that the petition asks for bread in the fullest sense, for the bread of life, does the antithesis between "for tomorrow" and "today" gain its full significance. This word "today," which stands at the end of the petition, gets the real stress. In a world enslaved under Satan, in a world where God is remote, in a world of hunger and thirst, the disciples of Jesus dare to utter this word "today"—even now, even here, already on this day, give us the bread of life. Jesus grants to them, as the children of God, the privilege of stretching forth their hands to grasp the glory of the consummation, to fetch it down, to "believe it down," to pray it down—right into their poor lives, even now, even here, today.

*Forgiveness.* Even now—this is also the meaning of the petition for forgiveness, "And forgive us our debts as we also herewith forgive our debtors." This request looks toward the great reckoning that the world is approaching, the disclosure of God's majesty in the final judgment. Jesus' disciples know how they are involved in sin and debt; they know that only God's gracious forgiveness can save them from the wrath to come. But they ask not only for mercy in the hour of the last judgment—rather, they ask, again, that God might grant them forgiveness already today. Through Jesus their Lord, they belong, as his disciples, to the age of salvation. The age of the Messiah is an age of forgiveness. Forgiveness is the one great gift of this age. "Grant us, dear Father," they pray, "this one great gift of the Messiah's time, already in this day and in this place."

This second "We-petition" also has two parts, two half-lines, like the petition for daily bread. There is an antithesis, contrasting "Thou" and "we": "forgive us our debts as we forgive our debtors." The second half-line about forgiving our debtors makes quite a striking reference to human activity. Such a reference occurs only at this point in the Lord's Prayer, so that one can see from this fact how important this second clause was to Jesus. The word "as" (in "as we forgive") does not imply a comparison. How could Jesus' disciples compare their poor forgiving with God's mercy? Rather, the "as" implies a causal effect; for as we have already seen, the correct translation from the Aramaic must be, "as we also herewith forgive our debtors." With these words the one who prays is reminded of the need to forgive. Jesus again and again declared this very point: you cannot ask God for forgiveness if you are not prepared to forgive. God can forgive only if we are ready to forgive. "Whenever you stand praying, forgive, if you have anything against anyone; so that your Father in heaven may also forgive you your trespasses" (Mark 11:25).

At Matthew 5:23-24, Jesus even goes so far as to say that the disciple is to interrupt the presentation of the offering for entreating God's forgiveness if it occurs to him that his brother holds something against him. He is to be reconciled with his brother before he completes the offering of his sacrifice. In these verses Jesus means to say that the request for God's forgiveness is false and cannot be heard by God if the disciple has not on his part previously cleared up his relationship with the brother. This willingness to forgive is, so to speak, the hand that Jesus' disciples reach out toward God's forgiveness. They say, "O Lord, we indeed belong to the age of the Messiah, to the age of forgiveness, and we are ready to pass on to others the forgiveness that we receive. Now grant us, dear Father, the gift of the age of salvation, your forgiveness. We stretch out our hands, forgive us our debts—even now, even here, already today."

Only when one observes that the two "We-petitions" are both directed toward the consummation and that they both implore its gifts for this present time, only then does the connection between the two "Thou-petitions" and the two "We-petitions" really become clear. The two "We-petitions" are the actualization of the "Thou-petitions." The "Thou-petitions" ask for the revelation of God's glory. The two "We-petitions" make bold to "pray down" this consummation, even here and even now.

### The Conclusion: The Petition for Preservation

Up to this point, the petitions have been in parallel to one another, the two "Thou-petitions" as well as the two "We-petitions." Moreover, the two "We-petitions" each consisted of two half-lines. Even the form, therefore, makes the concluding petition, which consists of only a single line, stand out as abrupt and harsh: "And let us not succumb to the trial." It also departs from the pattern of the previous petitions in that it is the only one formulated in the negative. But all that is intentional; as the contents show, this petition is supposed to stand out as abrupt.

Two remarks about the wording must be inserted here. The first concerns the Greek word *peirasmos*, which is usually rendered "temptation." "Lead us not into temptation" could be taken to imply that God himself tempts us. The

Letter of James has already rigorously rejected this misunderstanding when—evidently with direct reference to this final petition of the Lord's Prayer—it says, "No one, when tempted, should say, 'I am being tempted by God'; for God cannot be tempted by evil and he himself tempts no one" (James 1:13).

As a matter of fact, the translation "temptation" does not catch the sense of the concluding petition in its full depth. The Greek word *peirasmos* (like the Aramaic *nisyon* that lies behind it) can have two meanings: (1) temptation, that is, being led into sin; and (2) trial or testing, that is, faith or fidelity being put to the test. In the New Testament, where the word occurs twenty-one times, the meaning "temptation (into sin)" appears unequivocally in only one passage, 1 Timothy 6:9. In all the other passages the reference is to testing of faith or to God's fidelity being put to the test.

The closing petition of the Lord's Prayer also concerns the testing of faith. It does not have in mind the petty or major temptations of everyday life, but looks to the final, most severe proving of faith, that which lies ahead for Jesus' disciples at the disclosure of the mystery of evil, the revelation of the Antichrist, "desolating sacrilege," Satan in the place of God, the final persecution and imminent seduction of God's saints by pseudoprophets and false saviors. The final trial is apostasy!

The second observation about the wording of the closing petition concerns the verb, "lead us not." How this term "lead" is to be construed is shown by a very ancient Jewish evening prayer, which Jesus could have known and with which he perhaps makes a direct point of contact. The pertinent part (which recurs, incidentally, almost identically worded in the morning prayer) runs as follows:

> Lead me not into the power of transgression.
> And bring me not into the power of sin,
> and not into the power of iniquity,
> and not into the power of temptation,
> and not into the power of anything shameful. (*b. Ber.* 60b)

The juxtapositions of "transgression," "sin," "iniquity," "temptation," and "anything shameful," as well as the expression "bring into the power of," show that this Jewish evening prayer has in view not an unmediated action of God but his permission that allows something to happen. To put it in technical grammatical terms: the causative forms that are here translated "lead" and "bring" have a permissive nuance. The meaning is, "Do not permit that I fall into the hands of transgression, sin, iniquity, temptation, or anything shameful." This evening prayer thus prays for preservation from *succumbing* in temptation. This is also the sense of the concluding petition of the Lord's Prayer. We must render it, therefore, "Let us not succumb to the trial." This reference in the final petition of the Lord's Prayer is indeed not to preservation *from* the trial but to preservation *in* the trial. This conclusion is corroborated by a noncanonical saying of Jesus that, according to ancient tradition, Jesus spoke to his disciples on that last evening, prior to the prayer in Gethsemane:

> No one can obtain the kingdom of heaven
> who has not passed through testing.[20]

Here it is expressly stated that no disciple of Jesus will be spared the trial, and it is stressed that there is no exception; only he who conquers can obtain the kingdom. This saying also suggests that the concluding petition of the Lord's Prayer does not request that the one who prays might be spared the trial, but that God might help overcome it.

The final petition in the Lord's Prayer, therefore, says: "Let us not succumb to the trial." The trial of faith in the last, troubled times, on which Jesus, even in Gethsemane, warns the disciples, "Keep awake and pray that you do not succumb to the trial" (Mark 14:38a), consists of the danger of apostasy. Freely rendered, the closing petition says, "O Lord, preserve us from falling away." The Matthean tradition also understood the petition in this way when it added the petition about final deliverance from the power of evil, which seeks to plunge people into eternal ruin: "But deliver us from evil."

Now, perhaps, we understand the abruptness of this last petition and why it is so brief and harsh. Jesus has summoned his disciples to ask for the consummation, when God's name will be hallowed and his kingdom come. What is more, he has encouraged them in their petitions to "pray down" the gifts of the age of salvation into their own poor lives, even here and now. But with the soberness that characterizes all his words, Jesus warns his disciples of the danger of false enthusiasm when he calls them abruptly back to the reality of their own threatened existence by means of this concluding petition. This final petition is a cry out of the depths of distress, a resounding call for aid from a person who in affliction prays: "Dear Father, this one request grant us: preserve us from falling away from you."[21] It is surely no accident that this concluding petition has no parallels in the Old Testament.

## The Doxology

The doxology, "For yours is the kingdom and the power and the glory, forever, Amen," is lacking completely in Luke; and in Matthew it is absent from the oldest manuscripts. We encounter it first in the *Didache*.[22] But it would be a completely erroneous conclusion to suppose that the Lord's Prayer was ever prayed without some closing words of praise to God. In Palestinian practice it was completely unthinkable that a prayer would end with the words "the trial." In Judaism prayers were often concluded with a "seal," a sentence of praise freely formulated by the person who was praying.[23] This was doubtless also what Jesus intended with the Lord's Prayer and what the congregation did in the earliest period. Afterwards, when the Lord's Prayer began to be used increasingly in the service as a common prayer, it was felt necessary to establish a fixed formulation of the doxology.

If one ventures to summarize in *one* phrase the inexhaustible mystery of the few sentences in the Lord's Prayer, there is an expression preeminently suitable that New Testament research has especially busied itself with in recent decades. That phrase is "realized eschatology" (or "eschatology becoming actualized").[24] This expression denotes the age of salvation now being realized, the consummation bestowed in advance, the "in-breaking" of God's presence into our lives. Where people dare to pray in the name of Jesus to their heavenly Father with childlike trust that he might reveal his glory and that he might grant to them already today and in this place the bread of life and the blotting out of sins, there in the midst of the constant threat of failure and apostasy is realized, already now, the kingly rule of God over the life of his children.

Clement of Alexandria has preserved a saying of Jesus that is not included in the Gospels. It says, "Ask for the great things, so will God add to you the little things."[25] You are praying falsely, says the Lord. Always your prayers are moving in a circle around your own small "I," your own needs and troubles and desires. Ask for the great things—for God's almighty glory and kingdom, and that God's great gifts, the bread of life and the endless mercy of God, may be granted to you—even here, even now, already today. That does not mean that you may not bring your small personal needs before God, but they must not govern your prayer, for you are praying to your Father. He knows all. He knows the needs of his children before they ask him, and he adds to them his great gifts. Jesus says: Ask for the great things, so God will grant you the little things. The Lord's Prayer teaches us how to ask for the great things.

## NOTES

[1.] For Cyril's lectures in Greek and English, see *St. Cyril of Jerusalem's Lectures on the Christian Sacraments*, ed. F. L. Cross, Texts for Students 51 (London: SPCK, 1951). Another English translation is available in *Cyril of Jerusalem and Nemesius of Emesa*, ed. W. Telfer, LCC 4 (Philadelphia: Westminster, 1955).

2. T. W. Manson, "The Lord's Prayer," *BJRL* 38 (1955–56) 99–113, 436–48.

3. Jean-Paul Audet, *La Didaché: Instructions des Apôtres*, Etudes bibliques (Paris: Gabalda, 1958) 219. [Ed.] The most recent commentary estimates its date at 110–120, even though its sources are probably from the late first century: Kurt Niederwimmer, *The Didache*, trans. L. M. Maloney, Hermeneia (Minneapolis: Fortress Press, 1998) 52–54.

4. Alfred Seeberg, *Die vierte Bitte des Vaterunsers* (Rostock: Erben, 1914) 13–14; Manson, "Lord's Prayer," 101–2.

5. Manson, "Lord's Prayer," 101–2.

[6.] The Luther Bible and the *Zürcherbibel* were both originally produced during the Reformation, but they have been revised numerous times. The most recent versions are 1984 for the Luther Bible and 1988 for the *Zürcherbibel*.

[7.] The number of Greek New Testament manuscripts now available is more than 5,300; see Eldon J. Epp, "Textual Criticism (NT)," in *ABD* 6.412–35.

[8.] See Joachim Jeremias, *The Eucharistic Words of Jesus*, trans. N. Perrin (New York: Scribners, 1966; reprint, Philadelphia: Fortress Press, 1977).

[9.] Betz disagrees with Jeremias on this point, arguing that the versions in Matthew, Luke, and the *Didache* are all missing the transliterated Aramaic form one finds in Mark 14:36; Rom 8:15; and Gal 4:6. Hans Dieter Betz, *The Sermon on the Mount: A Commentary on the Sermon on the Mount, including the Sermon on the Plain (Matthew 5:3—7:27 and Luke 6:20-49)*, Hermeneia (Minneapolis: Fortress Press, 1995) 374–75. But see the more affirming view by John Ashton, "Abba," in *ABD* 1.7–8.

10. This was done in stages, as can be gathered from the fact that in Matthew the word "heaven/s" is in the plural in the address (Semitic usage), whereas it is in the singular in the third petition (Greek usage).

11. On the problem of the original Aramaic form and attempts at retranslation of the Lord's Prayer into Aramaic, see C. C. Torrey, "The Translations Made from the Original Aramaic Gospels," in *Studies in the History of Religions Presented to Crawford Howell Toy by Pupils, Colleagues and Friends* (New York: Macmillan, 1912) 309–17; C. F. Burney, "The Poetry of Our Lord (Oxford: Clarendon, 1925) 112–13; Gustaf Dalman, *Die Worte Jesu: mit Berücksichtigung des nachkanonischen jüdischen Schrifttums und der aramäischen Sprache erörtert*, rev. ed. (Leipzig: Hinrich, 1930; reprint, Darmstadt: Wissenschaftliche Buchgesellschaft, 1965) 283–365; ET: *The Words of Jesus*, trans. D. M. Kay (Edinburgh: T. & T. Clark, 1902); and Karl Georg Kuhn, *Achtzehngebet und Vaterunser und der Reim*, WUNT 1 (Tübingen: Mohr, 1950) 32–33. [Ed.] For a survey of Hebrew forms of the Lord's Prayer, see Jean Carmignac, "Hebrew Translations of the Lord's Prayer: An Historical Survey," in *Biblical and Near Eastern Studies: Essays in Honor of William Sanford LaSor*, ed. G. A. Tuttle (Grand Rapids: Eerdmans, 1978) 18–79.

12. Karl Heinrich Rengstorf, *Das Evangelium nach Lukas*, NTD 3 (Göttingen: Vandenhoeck & Ruprecht, 1962) 144.

[13.] "Hymn to the Moon-God," in *ANET*, 385. For an analysis of the gods as divine parents in ancient Mesopotamia, see Thorkild Jacobsen, *The Treasures of Darkness: A History of Mesopotamian Religion* (New Haven: Yale Univ. Press, 1976) 145–64.

[14.] See Gerhard Kittel, "αββα," in *TDNT* 1.5-6; and Gottlob Schrenk, "πατερ," in *TDNT* 5.945–1014, esp. 984–85.

[15.] *Ipsissima vox* is a Latin phrase meaning "actual voice." Jeremias uses this more general notion rather than the more specific *ipsissima verba*, "actual words."

16. One may translate the Aramaic in this way. The translation that is familiar to us remains possible: "Unless you turn and become like children. . . ."

[17.] This characterization of Judaism can hardly be sustained or affirmed. It is a piece of triumphalism that does not enhance Jeremias's argument.

[18.] See Morton S. Enslin, "Nazarenes, Gospel of the," in *IDB* 3.524; William L. Petersen, "Nazoraeans, Gospel of the," in *ABD* 4.1051–52. For an introduction and English translation, see John S. Kloppenborg, "Gospel of the Nazoreans," in *The Complete Gospels*, ed. R. J. Miller, rev. ed. (Sonoma, Calif.: Polebridge, 1994) 441–46.

[19.] For Jerome's quotation and comments, see Kloppenborg, "Nazoreans," 444.

[20.] Tertullian, *De baptismo* 20.2. For a discussion of this quotation, see Joachim Jeremias, *Unknown Sayings of Jesus*, trans. R. H. Fuller, rev. ed. (London: SPCK, 1964) 73–75.

21. See Heinz Schürmann, *Praying with Christ: The "Our Father" for Today*, trans. W. M. Ducey and A. Simon (New York: Herder & Herder, 1964) 89–90.

[22.] See Niederwimmer, *Didache*, 136–38.

23. Adolf Schlatter, *Der Evangelist Matthaeus: Seine Sprache, Sein Ziel, Seine Selbstaendigkeit. Ein Kommentar zum Ersten Evangelium*, 4th ed. (Stuttgart: Calwer, 1957) 217.

[24.] The phrase "realized eschatology" is most closely associated with C. H. Dodd. Jeremias preferred the English phrase "eschatology becoming actualized" for the German expression *sich realisierende Eschatologie*.

[25.] See Jeremias, *Unknown Sayings*, 98–100; Clement of Alexandria, *Stromata* 1.24.258.2; also quoted by Origen, Eusebius, and Ambrose.

# 4

# The Central Message
# of the New Testament

## 'ABBA'

### *God as "Father" in the Old Testament*

From earliest times, the Near East was familiar with the mythological idea that the deity is the father of humanity or of certain humans. Peoples, tribes, and families picture themselves as being the offspring of a divine ancestor. Particularly, it is the king as representative of his people who enjoys a special share of the dignity and power of a divine father. Whenever the word "father" is used for a deity in this connection, it implies fatherhood in the sense of unconditional and irrevocable authority.

All this is mere commonplace in the history of religion. But it is less well known that already very early the word "father" as an epithet for the deity repeatedly carries a specific overtone. In a famous Sumerian and Akkadian hymn from Ur, the moon-god Sin is invoked as "Begetter, merciful in his disposing, who holds in his hand the life of the whole land."[1] And it is said of the Sumerian-Babylonian god Ea:

> His wrath is like the deluge,
> his being reconciled like a merciful father.[2]

For those in the ancient Near East, the word "father," as applied to God, thus encompasses, from earliest times, something of what the word "mother" signifies among us.

This is even truer of the Old Testament. God is seldom spoken of as "Father," in fact, only fourteen times. All of these occurrences, however, are important. First of all, God is honored as the creator when called "Father":

> Is not he your father, who created you,
>> who made you and established you? (Deut 32:6)

> Have we not all one father?
> Has not one God created us? (Mal 2:10)

As the creator, God is the Lord. He can expect to be honored by obedience. On the other hand, being Father, God is also thought of as merciful:

> As a father has compassion for his children,
>> so Yahweh has compassion for those who fear him.
> For he knows how we were made;
>> he remembers that we are dust. (Ps 103:13-14)

Just because God is the creator, he is full of fatherly indulgence for the weaknesses of his children.

It is quite obvious that in all these references the Old Testament reflects the ancient Near Eastern concept of divine fatherhood. Still there are fundamental differences. Not the least of them is the fact that in the Old Testament God is not the ancestor or progenitor but the creator. Even more important is the fact that in the Old Testament divine fatherhood is related to Israel alone in a quite unparalleled manner. Israel has a particular relationship to God. Israel is God's firstborn, chosen out of all peoples (Deut 14:1-2). Moreover, this election of Israel as God's firstborn son was thought of as being rooted in a concrete historical action, the exodus from Egypt. Combining God's fatherhood with a historical action involves a profound revision of the concept of God as Father. The certainty that God is Father and Israel his son is grounded not in mythology but in a unique act of salvation by God, which Israel had experienced in history.

It was not until the prophets, however, that the concept of God as Father gained its full significance in the Old Testament. Again and again, the prophets are obliged to say that Israel repays God's fatherly love with constant ingratitude. Most of the prophetic statements about God as Father passionately and emphatically point to the contradiction that manifests itself between Israel's sonship and its godlessness.

Have you not just now called to me,

> "My Father, you are the friend of my youth—
>> will he be angry forever,
>> will he be indignant to the end?"
> This is how you have spoken,
>> but you have done all the evil that you could (Jer 3:4-5)

I thought
>> how would I set you among my children,
> and give you a pleasant land,
>> the most beautiful heritage of all the nations.
> And I thought you would call me, My Father,
>> and would not turn from following me.
> Instead, as a faithless wife leaves her husband,
>> so you have been faithless to me, O house of Israel,
>> says Yahweh. (Jer 3:19-20)

A son honors his father,
>> and servants their master.
> If then I am a father, where is the honor due me?
>> And if I am a master, where is the respect due me?
>> (Mal 1:6)

Israel's constant answer to this call to repentance is the cry: "You are my [or: our] Father" (*'abinu 'attah*). In Trito-Isaiah this cry is elaborated into a final appeal for God's mercy and forgiveness:

Look down from heaven and see,
>> from your holy and glorious habitation.
> Where are your zeal and your might?
>> The yearning of your heart and your compassion?
>> They are withheld from me.
> For you are our father (*'abinu 'attah*),
>> though Abraham does not know us
>> and Israel does not acknowledge us;
> You, O Yahweh, are our father ('abinu 'attah);
>> our Redeemer from of old is your name. (Isa 63:15-16)

Yet, O Yahweh, you are our Father (*'abinu 'attah*);
>> we are the clay, and you are our potter;
>> we are all the work of your hand.
> Do not be exceedingly angry, O Yahweh,
>> and do not remember iniquity forever. (Isa 64:7-8)

God answers this appeal of Israel with forgiveness. Hosea 11:1-11 draws a touching picture of this. God is compared to a father who taught his little son Ephraim to walk and carried him in his arms:

> Yet it was I who taught Ephraim to walk,
>> I took them up in my arms . . .
> How can I give you up, Ephraim?
>> How can I hand you over, O Israel? (Hos 11:3, 8)

Similarly, the prophet Jeremiah has found the most moving expressions for God's forgiveness:

> With weeping they shall come,
>> and with consolations I will lead them back,
> I will let them walk by brooks of water,
>> in a straight path in which they shall not stumble;
> for I have become a father to Israel,
>> and Ephraim is my firstborn. (Jer 31:9)

God's fatherly mercy exceeds all human comprehension:

> Is Ephraim my dear son?
>> Is he the child I delight in? . . .
> Therefore I am deeply moved for him;
>> I will surely have mercy on him, says Yahweh. (Jer 31:20)

This is the final word of the Old Testament with regard to divine fatherhood: the "must" of God's incomprehensible mercy and forgiveness.

## Palestinian Judaism

Like the Old Testament, Palestinian Judaism in the time before Jesus was very reluctant to speak of God as Father. In the whole of the Qumran literature, for instance, which must have been composed before 68 C.E., there is just one single passage to be found where the name "father" is applied to God:

> My father did not know me,
>> and my mother abandoned me to you.
> For you are a father (*'attah 'ab*)
>> to all the sons of your truth. (1QH 17.35-36).

Rabbinical Judaism used the epithet somewhat more freely, though not abundantly. If we inquire what Jesus' Jewish contemporaries meant to express by giving God the name of Father, two characteristics emerge.

First, no one who is familiar with Judaism during this period will be astonished to find that the obligation to obey the heavenly father is vigorously stressed. The rabbis teach that God extends his fatherhood only to those who fulfill the Law (*torah*). He is the Father of those who do his will, of those who are just. Nevertheless, again and again the tremendous assurance of the prophets recurs that God's fatherly love is boundless and exceeds all human guilt. When Rabbi Judah (c. 150 C.E.) taught:

> If you behave like children,
>     you are called children.
> If you do not behave like children,
>     you are not called children.

His colleague and antagonist Rabbi Meir contradicted him with the bold, concise sentence: "Either way—you are called children" (*b. Qidd.* 36a [*Bar.*]). God's fatherly love is his first and his last word, however great the children's guilt may be.

The second characteristic of Jewish statements of this period about God's fatherhood is that God is repeatedly spoken of as the Father of the individual Israelite, and that he is addressed as Father in liturgical prayers: "Our Father, our King" (*'abinu malkenu*). Thus a prayer from the Mishnah that could easily stem from the days of Jesus reads:

> Our Father, our King,
> for the sake of our fathers,
> who trusted in you,
> and whom you taught the statutes of life—
> have mercy upon us and teach us. (*m. Tamid* 5.1)[3]

This is new as compared with the Old Testament. Several things must not be overlooked here, however. First, Hebrew is used, the sacred language that was not employed in everyday speech. Second, the dual address, "Our Father, our King," underscores God's majesty as a king as much as his fatherhood, or even more so. Third, it is the community as a whole that addresses God as "our Father."

To date, nobody has produced one single instance in Palestinian Judaism where God is addressed as "my Father" by an individual person.[4] There are a few examples in Hellenistic Judaism, but these are due to Greek influence. From Palestinian writings, only one passage may be quoted, namely, two related verses from Sirach 23 (dating from the beginning of the second century B.C.E.). These are, however, unfortunately only extant in Greek. Here we read, "O Lord, Father and God of my life" (Sirach 23:4). These two verses would be the only exception to the rule, and we would praise them as a prelude to the gospel, were it not that some thirty years ago a Hebrew paraphrase of this passage was discovered. Here the address is not "O Lord, Father" but "O God of my father."[5] It can hardly be doubted that this was the wording of the address in the original Hebrew text, for the designation of God as "God of my father," stemming from Exodus 15:2, was widespread and occurs elsewhere in Sirach. This means that there is no evidence so far that anyone addressed God as "my Father" in Palestinian Judaism of the first millennium.

### 'Abba' *in the Prayers of Jesus*

But Jesus did just this. To his disciples it must have been something quite extraordinary that Jesus addressed God as "my Father." Moreover, not only do the four Gospels attest that Jesus used this address, but they report unanimously that he did so in all his prayers.[6] There is only one prayer of Jesus in which "my Father" is lacking. That is the cry from the cross: "My God, my God, why have you forsaken me?" (Mark 15:34 / Matt 27:46), quoting Psalm 22:1.

Still, we have not yet said everything. The most remarkable thing is that when Jesus addressed God as his Father in prayer he used the Aramaic word *'abba'*. Mark states this explicitly in his report on the prayer in Gethsemane: "'*Abba*', Father, for you all things are possible; remove this cup from me; yet, not what I want, but what you want" (Mark 14:36). That Jesus used the same word *'abba'* in his other prayers as well is proven by a comparison of the different forms the address "father" takes in Greek. Besides the correct Greek vocative form *pater* (father)[7] or *pater mou* (my father),[8] we find the nominative *ho patēr* used as a vocative that is not correct Greek usage.[9] This oscillation between vocative and nominative that occurs even in one and the same logion (Matt 11:25, 26 / Luke 10:21) cannot be explained without taking into account that the word *'abba'* —as we shall presently see—was current in first-century Palestinian Aramaic not only as an address, but also for "the father" (the emphatic state; *status emphaticus*). Finally, besides Mark 14:36 and the variation of the address "father" in Greek, we have a third piece of evidence to prove that Jesus said *'abba'* when he prayed. It consists of two passages in Paul: Romans 8:15 and Galatians 4:6. They inform us that the Christian communities used the cry *'Abba' ho patēr* ('Abba', Father) and considered this an utterance brought forth by the Holy Spirit. This applies to the Pauline (Galatians) as well as the non-Pauline (Romans) communities, and there can be no doubt at all that this early Christian cry is an echo of Jesus' own praying.

This is without analogy in Jewish prayers of the first millennium C.E. Nowhere in the literature of the prayers of ancient Judaism—an immense treasure all too little explored—is this invocation of God as *'Abba'* to be found, either in the liturgical or in informal prayers.

Only one passage in late Jewish literature uses the word *'abba'* in a certain connection with God. This is a story that relates an event that happened toward the end of the first century B.C.E. It deals with Ḥanin ha-Neḥba, a man reputed for his successful prayers for rain, and reads:

> When the world was in need of rain, our teachers used to send the schoolchildren to him, who grasped the hem of his coat and implored him: "Daddy, Daddy, give us rain" (*'Abba', 'abba', hab lan miṭra'*). He said to Him [God]: "Master of the world, grant it [the rain] for the sake of these who are not yet able to distinguish between an *'abba'* who has the power to give rain, and an *'abba'* who has not. (*b. Ta'an.* 23b)

At first sight it would seem as if here we have one instance in which God is called *'Abba'*. But two things must be observed. First, the word *'abba'* is applied to God in almost a joking manner. Ḥanin appeals to God's mercy by adopting the cry "Daddy, Daddy, give us rain," which the children repeat after him in a chorus, calling God an "*'Abba'* who has the power to give rain," as children would in their own language. The second point is still more important. Ḥanin by no means addresses God as *'Abba'*. On the contrary, his address is "Master of the world." No doubt the story is something like a prelude to Jesus' assertion that the heavenly Father knows what his children need (Matt 6:32 par.), that he sends rain on the just and the unjust (Matt 5:45), and that he gives good things to his children who ask him (Matt 7:11 / Luke 11:13). But it does not give us the looked-for attestation of *'abba'* as an address to God. The fact remains unshaken that for this usage we have no evidence at all in Judaism.

This is a result of fundamental importance. Jewish prayers on the one hand do not contain a single example of *'abba'* as an address for God. Jesus, on the other hand, always used it when he prayed (with the exception of the cry from the cross, Mark 15:34). This means that we have here an unequivocal characteristic of the unique way in which Jesus expressed himself, of his *ipsissima vox*.

The reason Jewish prayers do not address God as *'Abba'* is disclosed when one considers the linguistic background of the word. Originally, *'abba'* was a babbling sound. The Talmud says, "When a child experiences the taste of wheat [that is, when it is weaned] it learns to say *'abba'* and *'immah'*" (*b. Ber.* 40a [*Bar.*]; *Sanh.* 70b [*Bar.*]); that is, "Dada" and "Mama" are the first words the child utters. And the church fathers John Chrysostom, Theodor of Mopsuestia, and Theodoret of Cyrrhus—all three of them born in Antioch of well-to-do parents, but in all probability raised by Syrian nurses—tell us from their own experience, that little children used to call their fathers *'abba'*. When I started this study, which occupied me for quite a few years, I thought that it was just this babbling sound that Jesus adopted.

But soon I noticed that this conclusion was too rash, for it overlooked the fact that already in pre-Christian times this word, which surely originated from the idiom of the small child, had vastly extended its range of meaning in Palestinian Aramaic. *'Abba'* supplanted the older form *'abi* as an address to the father that was used in Palestinian Aramaic at least until the second century B.C.E., as we have learned from the Dead Sea Scrolls. *'Abba'* furthermore took over the connotations of "my father" and of "the father"; it even occasionally replaced "his father" and "our father." In this way, the word no longer remained restricted to the idiom of little children. Grown sons and daughters called their fathers *'abba'* as well (see Luke 15:21) and only on formal occasions resorted to "Sir" (Greek *kyrie*; see Matt 21:29). But in spite of this development, the origin of the word in the language of infants never falls into oblivion.

We are now in a position to say why *'abba'* is not used in Jewish prayers as an address to God: to a Jewish mind it would have been irreverent and therefore unthinkable to call God by this familiar word.[10] It was something new, something unique and unheard of, that Jesus dared to take this step and to speak with God as a child speaks with his father, simply, intimately, securely. There is no doubt then that the *'Abba'* that Jesus uses to address God reveals the very basis of his communion with God.

### The Fatherhood of God in the Gospels

Is this childlike address to God to be regarded as a last stage in the general development of human relations with God, or is there more in it? We shall get an answer when we broaden our survey of the sources.

Until now we have limited ourselves to the address of God as Father in the prayers of Jesus. We are led a step deeper when we turn to the sayings in which Jesus speaks of God as Father. That is to say, we turn our attention from the address "my Father" to the designation of God as Father.

No less than one hundred and seventy times do we encounter in the Gospels the word Father for God in the mouth of Jesus. At first glance there does not appear to be the least doubt that for Jesus "Father" was *the* designation for God. But is this really true? When we classify the passages according to the five strata of tradition represented in the Gospels, the following pattern emerges (counting the synoptic parallels only once and excluding the address "Father"):

| Mark | 3 |
| Sayings common to | |
| Matthew and Luke (so-called Q) | 4 |
| Sayings special to Luke | 4 |
| Sayings special to Matthew | 31 |
| John | 100 |

This survey shows that there existed an increasing tendency to introduce the designation of God as Father into the sayings of Jesus. Mark, the sayings tradition (Q), and the material peculiar to Luke all agree in reporting that Jesus used the word "Father" for God only in a few instances. In Matthew there is a noticeable increase, and in John "Father" has become almost a synonym for God. Apparently Jesus employed the name "Father" only on special occasions. But why?

The few examples that the oldest strata of tradition record for the designation of God as Father fall into two classes: first, a group in which Jesus speaks of God as "your Father"; and second, a group in which Jesus calls him "my Father." The "your Father" sayings picture God as the Father who knows what his children need (Matt 6:32 / Luke 12:30), who is merciful (Luke 6:36) and unlimited in goodness (Matt 5:45), who can forgive (Mark 11:25), and whose good pleasure it is to grant the kingdom to the little flock (Luke 12:32). In the oldest strata of tradition these "your Father" sayings seem to have been all addressed to the disciples. They are one characteristic of the instruction (*didachē*) of disciples, the esoteric teaching of Jesus. To those outside the circle, Jesus seems to have spoken only in parables and similes about God as Father.

Of these esoteric sayings the most important is:

> All things have been handed over to me by my Father;
> and no one knows the Son except the Father,
> and no one knows the Father except the Son
> and anyone to whom the Son chooses to reveal him.
>
> (Matt 11:27 / Luke 10:22)

Karl von Hase, a professor of church history at Jena, Germany, in the nineteenth century, coined the famous metaphor in his book on the history of Jesus that this Synoptic saying "gives the impression of a thunderbolt fallen from the Johannine sky."[11] Two things above all in this passage appeared Johannine: first, the phrase about mutual knowledge that was regarded as a technical term drawn from Hellenistic mysticism; and second, the designation of Jesus as "the Son," which is characteristic of Johannine Christology. For a long time it was considered certain that Matthew 11:27 was a product of Hellenistic Christianity.

Not so long ago, however, the tide began to turn. It was increasingly recognized that, as T. W. Manson put it, "the passage is full of Semitic turns of phrase and certainly Palestinian in origin"; or, as Wilfred L. Knox said, it is "purely Semitic."[12] Indeed, language, style, and structure clearly assign the saying to a Semitic-speaking milieu.[13] The two objections just mentioned can be answered on simple linguistic grounds. Already in 1898, Gustaf Dalman drew attention to the fact that Hebrew and Aramaic lack the reciprocal pronoun: "one another," "each other."[14] Instead, they employ a roundabout way of expression when they want to describe reciprocal action. Further, we must remember that in Aramaic, especially in similes and comparisons, the definite article is quite often used in a generic sense. Taking these two facts into account, we must translate Matthew 11:27: "As only a father knows his son, so only a son knows his father."

This means that the passage neither speaks about a mystical union (*unio mystica*) brought about by mutual knowledge, nor does it use the Christological title "the Son." Rather, Jesus' words simply express a plain, everyday experience: only father and son truly know each other. If this is true, then Matthew 11:27 is not a Johannine verse amid the synoptic material, but rather one of those sayings from which Johannine theology developed. Without such points of departure within the synoptic tradition, it would be an eternal puzzle how Johannine theology could have originated at all.[15]

The saying in Matthew 11:27 is a four-line couplet. The first line indicates the theme: "All things have been handed over to me by my Father." My father has granted me full knowledge of him, says the first line. The three remaining lines elucidate this theme by means of the father-son comparison. Freely paraphrased, they say: "And because only a father and son truly know each other, a son can reveal to others the innermost thoughts of his father. Now one has to know that the father-son comparison is familiar to Palestinian apocalyptic as an illustration of how revelation is transmitted. "Every secret did I reveal to him as a father," God says in *3 Enoch* 48:7. And in another passage, a rabbi reports: "The heavenly messenger showed me the things that were woven into the heavenly curtain . . . by pointing with his finger as a father who teaches his son the letters of the Torah" (*3 Enoch* 45:1-2). So if Jesus interprets the theme "All things have been handed over to me by my Father" with the aid of this father-son comparison, what he wants to convey in the disguise of an everyday simile is this: As a father who personally devotes himself to explaining to his son the letters of the Torah, so God has transmitted to me the revelation of himself; and, therefore, I alone can pass on to others the real knowledge of God.

This saying in which Jesus bears witness to himself and his mission does not stand isolated in the Gospels.[16] Here we quote only a variant to Matthew 11:26, which was current in the second century among the Marcosians, a Gnostic sect, and which goes back to an old Aramaic tradition. According to this reading, Jesus cried out: "O my father, that good pleasure was granted me before you!"[17] This variant form of the exclamation in Matthew 11:26 may well be secondary. Nevertheless, it strikes the original note of Jesus' joy over the revelation granted to him, a joy that also permeates our passage. "O 'Abba', that good pleasure was granted me before you!"

Thus when Jesus spoke of God as "my Father," he was referring not to a familiarity and intimacy with God available to anyone, but to a unique revelation that was bestowed upon him. He bases his authority on the fact that God has graciously endowed him with the full revelation, revealing himself to him as only a father can reveal himself to his son. 'Abba', then, is a word that conveys revelation. It represents the center of Jesus' awareness of his mission.

If one looks for foreshadowing of this unique relation to God as Father, one must go as far back as the prophecy given to Nathan concerning David: "I will be his father, and he shall be my son" (2 Sam 7:14 / 1 Chron 17:13), and to words about the king in the Psalms:

> He shall cry to me, "You are my Father,
>     my God and the Rock of my salvation."
> And I will make him the first-born,
>     the highest of the kings of the earth.
>                     (Ps 89:26-27; see 2:7)

From the Pseudepigrapha we may quote the promise given to the priestly Messiah, that God would speak to him "with a fatherly voice" (*T. Levi* 18:6) and the affirmation extending to the Messiah from Judah that "the blessings of the holy father" shall be poured out over him (*T. Jud.* 24:2). This means that this "my Father" of Jesus is foreshadowed only within the context of the messianic expectation. Matthew 11:27, then, implies that these promises were fulfilled in Jesus.

### The Lord's Prayer

It is only against this background that we can understand the deepest meaning of the Lord's Prayer.[18] It is handed down to us in two forms: the shorter one in Luke 11:2-4, and the longer one in Matthew 6:9-13. Whereas no one would have dared to shorten this central passage, it is easy to conceive of an expansion of the passage in conjunction with its liturgical usage. The shorter Lukan version must then be the older one. Here the address is simply *pater*, the equivalent of 'Abba'.

In order to understand what this address meant for the disciples, we have to refer to the situation in which Jesus gave his disciples the Our Father. According to Luke 11:1, they had asked, "Lord, teach us to pray." One is to recognize that this request implied the desire of the disciples to have a prayer of their own, just as the followers of John the Baptist, the Pharisees, and the Essenes had their own prayers, tokens of their communion. "Lord, teach us to pray" means then: "Lord, give us a prayer that will be the sign and token of your followers."

Jesus fulfills this request, and in so doing he first and foremost authorizes his disciples to follow him in saying *'Abba'*. He gives them this address as the token of their discipleship. By the authorization that they too may invoke God as *'Abba'*, he lets them participate in his own communion with God. He even goes as far as to say that only he who can repeat this childlike *'Abba'* shall enter into the kingdom of God.[19] This address, *'Abba'*, when spoken by the disciples, is a sharing in the revelation; it is actualized eschatology. It is the presence of the kingdom even here, even now. It is a fulfillment, granted in advance, of the promise:

> I shall be their father
> and they my children.
> They all shall be called
> children of the living God. (*Jub.* 1:24-25)

This is the way Paul understood the address when he says twice that it is proof of the possession of sonship and of the Spirit, when a Christian repeats this one word *'Abba'* (Rom 8:15; Gal 4:6). The ancient Christian liturgies show their awareness of the greatness of this gift in that they preface the Lord's Prayer with the words "We *make bold* to say: 'Our Father.'"

## Conclusion

With all this we are facing a conclusion of fundamental importance. It has been widely maintained that we know scarcely anything about the historical Jesus. We know him only from the Gospels, which are not historical accounts but rather confessions of faith. We know only the Christ of the Kerygma, where Jesus is clad in the garb of myth; one need only think of the many miracles attributed to him. What we discover, when we apply historical criticism in analyzing the sources, is a powerful prophet, but a prophet who completely remained within the limits of Judaism. This prophet may have historical interest, but he has not and cannot have any significance for the Christian faith. What matters is the Christ of the kerygma. Christianity began at Easter.

But if it is true—and the testimony of the sources is quite unequivocal—that *'Abba'* as an address to God is an authentic and original utterance of Jesus (*ipsissima vox*), and that this *'Abba'* implies the claim of a unique revelation and a unique authority—if all this is true, then the position regarding the historical Jesus just described is untenable. For with *'Abba'* we are behind the kerygma. We are confronted with something new and unheard of that breaks through the limits of Judaism. Here we see who the historical Jesus was: the man who had the power to address God as *'Abba'* and who included the sinners and the publicans in the kingdom by authorizing them to repeat this one word, "*'Abba'*, dear Father."

## THE SACRIFICIAL DEATH OF JESUS

### *The Atonement in Hebrews and 1 Peter*

Of all New Testament writings, the Letter to the Hebrews provides us with the most extensive interpretation of the cross.[20] This letter—actually the oldest Gentile Christian sermon preserved (13:22)—distinguishes between elementary instruction (the "first principles" 5:12) and deeper knowledge (called "maturity" in 6:1), in other words, between *exoteric* and *esoteric* teaching. The former contained instruction about baptism and the end of the times; it was, in short, the substance of what catechumens had to learn (see Heb 6:1-2). Esoteric teaching, on the other hand, concerns itself with the Eucharist[21] and, above all, with the doctrine of the self-sacrifice of Christ, the heavenly high priest. The explanation of this doctrine forms the central part of the letter (7:1—10:18).

In order to illustrate the saving power of Christ's death, Hebrews draws upon the ritual for the Day of Atonement, celebrated on 10 Tishri every autumn, as laid down in Leviticus 16. The Day of Atonement, Israel's great day of repentance and reconciliation, was the only day during the entire year on which a human being was allowed to enter the Holy of Holies. Trembling, because even a minor deviation from the prescribed ritual would entail a terrible death, the high priest penetrated into the darkness behind the curtain to offer that precious blood that was to remove all sins. The Letter to the Hebrews makes this ritual a type of the atoning work of Christ in two ways.

First (here Hebrews is dependent upon traditional ideas), Christ is compared to the faultless victim, who through his vicarious death assures forgiveness and full communion with God. Second, elaborating an expression from Psalm 110:4, Hebrews also depicts Christ as the eternal, sinless high priest who, having atoned for sin once and for all, remains perpetually in the presence of God and intercedes with sympathy for his people (Heb 7:25; 9:24; see also 2:18; 4:14-16).

This Christology of Hebrews is a very impressive attempt to lead the church to an understanding of the mystery of the cross by means of a typological interpretation of Leviticus 16. Stripped of its imagery, this interpretation means Good Friday is *the* Day of Atonement of the New Covenant, of which all the Days of Atonement, repeated year after year, were but types and patterns. The benefits of this new, and final, Day of Atonement are twofold. First, Christ's vicarious, sinless death answers the human cry for forgiveness—once and for all (Heb 7:27; 9:12; 10:10). Second, actualizing this reconciliation, Christ, himself tempted and afflicted while on earth, intercedes in heaven for his tempted and afflicted church.

When we turn to 1 Peter we find that quite different imagery is used to interpret Jesus' death, namely, the doctrine of Christ's descent into and preaching in Hades (1 Peter 3:19-20; 4:6).[22] In order to understand this doctrine, it must be observed that it has an antitype in the Book of *1 Enoch*, which received its present shape after the invasion of Palestine by the Parthians in 37 B.C.E. Chapters 12–16 of this book describe how Enoch is sent to the fallen angels of Genesis 6 to convey to them the message that they will "find no peace and no forgiveness" (*1 Enoch* 12:5). Stricken with terror, they ask Enoch to draw up a petition in which they implore God's indulgence and forgiveness. Enoch is then lifted up to God's fiery throne and receives God's answer that he must dispatch to the fallen sons of God. It consists of one short clause of five words only, the terrible sentence: "You will have no peace" (16:3).

It can hardly be doubted that the doctrine of Christ's descent into Hades is modeled upon this myth from *1 Enoch*. But whereas Enoch's message spells out the impossibility of forgiveness, Christ announces something different: the good news (1 Peter 4:6). "The righteous one died for the unrighteous" (3:18). His atoning death means salvation even for those who were hopelessly lost.

Both Hebrews and 1 Peter intend to elucidate what happened on Good Friday, but in doing so they resort to utterly different illustrations. Hebrews speaks of Jesus *ascending* into heaven in order to offer his blood in the heavenly Holy of Holies, whereas 1 Peter speaks of Jesus *descending* into the blackest depths of Hades in order to preach to the "spirits in prison." Ascent and descent are two parallel attempts to bring out the meaning of Good Friday. The two representations are different from each other: Hebrews using cultic imagery, 1 Peter employing mythological imagery. As far as the local aspect is concerned, they even stand opposed to each other. This is a wholesome warning against overestimating the importance of the imagery involved. What matters is the point at which they agree. Both wish to express one and the same message: the atoning power of Jesus' death is inexhaustible and boundless.

## Paul

Both Hebrews and 1 Peter reveal themselves as dependent in many ways upon the theology of Paul. We now turn our attention to his letters as we trace our way back through the New Testament. Here we meet with a new situation. It is not as though Paul had something to say about Christ's death that differs in content from the post-Pauline writings. On the contrary, the stability of content in spite of varying forms is one of the most prominent characteristics of our subject throughout the New Testament. The difference between Paul and, let us say, the Letter to the Hebrews is not one of opinion but of atmosphere. Hebrews endeavors to explain and amplify the mystery of the cross by a profound and well-balanced array of typological arguments, the fruit of an intensive theological reflection. On the other hand, when we read what Paul writes about the same subject, we still get a feeling of how he had to wrestle with the problem of getting this much-debated core of his message across to his hearers.

Let me illustrate this by an example that gives us a glimpse of how the interpretation of the cross, later a firmly established part of the church's tradition, had to be intensely fought for in the beginning. I mean Galatians 3:13: "Christ became a curse for us," or rather (if we observe that "became" is a circumlocution for the action of God, and that "curse" is a metonym for "the cursed one") "God made Christ a cursed one for our sake." This sentence from Galatians—in which Paul applies Deuteronomy 21:23 ("A hanged man is accursed by God") to Christ—is so familiar to us that we no longer sense its original offensiveness. We should—perhaps if we noted that not one other New Testament writer ever dared utter anything that even remotely resembles this statement of Paul's. The only explanation of this shocking phrase "God made Christ a cursed one" is that it originated in the time before the episode on the Damascus road.[23] Jesus of Nazareth, a man ostensibly accursed by God—that was why Saul persecuted him in the guise of his followers, why he blasphemed him (1 Tim 1:13) and tried to compel blasphemy from his disciples (Acts 26:11), namely the cry *Anathema Jesus*—"Jesus be cursed" (1 Cor 12:3).[24] But then, on the Damascus road, the accursed one appeared before Paul in divine glory. After this experience, Paul still went on saying, "God made Christ a cursed one," but now he added two words: "for us" or "for me" (Gal 2:20). From now on "for us" was to be the heart of his existence. By an increasing number of comparisons and images, he tries to make his hearers and readers understand the meaning of this "for us," that is, the idea of Christ's vicarious death. Among them, four themes may easily be identified.

First, there is the cultic theme that was suggested to Paul by Christian tradition. In 1 Corinthians 5:7 he says: "You are free from leaven. For Christ has been sacrificed as our Passover lamb." To be a Christian, Paul says, is to live at

Passover time, to stand in the light of Easter morning, in a new life—this Passover began when our Passover lamb was sacrificed on Calvary. Along with this comparison of Christ to the Passover lamb—also found in 1 Peter and the Gospel of John—Paul uses other comparisons drawn from cultic language. Thus, in Romans 3:25, he compares Christ with the sacrifice offered on the Day of Atonement; in Romans 8:3 with the sin-offering; in Ephesians 5:2 with the burnt offering. In each case the treatment of Jesus' death in terms of sacrifice has the intention of expressing the fact that Jesus died without sin in substitution for our sins. His death is the sum and the end of all sacrifices prescribed by the Old Testament ritual. It is the one sacrifice for the sins of all humanity.

A second theme used by Paul to illustrate how Christ took our place is borrowed from criminal law. All those passages referring to Isaiah 53, the chapter about the Suffering Servant who carried the punishment inflicted because of our transgressions, belong here, as for instance Romans 4:25: "who was handed over to death for our trespasses."[25] A particularly impressive image illustrating how Christ suffered the death penalty that we deserved is used in Colossians 2:14: "[God was] erasing the record that stood against us with its legal demands. He set this aside, nailing it to the cross." When a man was crucified, a tablet was affixed over his head—the so-called *titulus*—which he had carried around his neck on his way to the place of execution. The crimes for which he had been sentenced were inscribed on this *titulus*. Above Jesus' head also hangs a *titulus*. "But do you not see," says Paul, "that there is a hand that removes this *titulus* and replaces it with another one, with lines of writing crowded upon it? You will have to draw near if you want to decipher this new *titulus*—it is your sins and mine that are inscribed upon it."

Besides the cultic and the legal themes, Paul has taken a third theme from the institution of slavery. The key terms are "to buy" (1 Cor 6:20; 7:23), "to redeem" (Gal 3:13; 4:5), and "with a price" (1 Cor 6:20; 7:23). Christ redeemed us from slavery through his death. What Paul means is the dramatic act of entering into slavery in order to redeem a slave. It is this self-sacrifice out of love to which Paul alludes when he says in 1 Corinthians 13:3: "If I give away all my possessions, and if I deliver my body to be burned (that is, branded with the slave-mark), but do not have love, I gain nothing." We know from the *First Letter of Clement* (96 C.E.) that such extreme expressions of brotherly love did in fact occur in the earliest churches (*1 Clem.* 55.2). That, says Paul, is what Christ did for us. We were slaves of sin (Rom 3:9 and others), of the law (Gal 4:5), of God's curse (Gal 3:13). The crucified Lord took our place as a slave of these powers in order to redeem us legitimately (1 Cor 6:20; 7:23). To grasp the wonderful ring that the word "redemption" had in the ears of the slaves who belonged to the earliest Christian communities, we must be mindful of the terrible condition of slaves in antiquity who were helplessly exposed to the whims and caprices of their owners and were forced to work themselves to death in mines or on the galleys.

The last of our four themes is the ethical substitution consisting in Christ's vicarious obedience, of which—if I am not mistaken—there are only two occurrences. The first is Romans 5:18-19. Here, in two antithetic phrases of similar structure, Paul contrasts the universal effects of Adam's transgression with Christ's act of obedience: "by the one man's obedience (that is, because he kept the commandments in our place, which we should have kept) the many will be made righteous." The second instance is Galatians 4:4-5: "God sent his son, born of a woman, born under the law, in order to redeem those who were under the law, so that we might receive adoption as children."

The images may be different, but one and the same intention underlies these four themes: Paul wants to illustrate the "for us," the sinless one taking the place of the sinners. He takes the very place of the ungodly (Rom 5:6), of the enemies of God (5:10), of the world opposed to God (2 Cor 5:19). In this way the boundless omnipotence of God's all-inclusive love reveals itself (Rom 5:8). Christ's vicarious death on the cross is the actualization of God's love.

## The Earliest Churches

Going back one step further, we now direct our attention to the earliest churches before Paul. Here the difficulty arises that the earliest churches have left us no written statements. And yet we may say with certainty that the interpretation of the meaning of the cross was a point of major concern even for the Christian community. From the very day of Easter, the historical situation forced them to give an answer to the mystery of the cross.

To the ancients the cross was the symbol not only of the most horrible sufferings, but also of utmost infamy (Heb 12:2). In addition, as we have seen, Jewish sentiment concluded from Deuteronomy 21:23 that this form of capital punishment, unknown to Israel, was a token of God's curse. How then could it happen that he whom God had acknowledged through the resurrection should have died under God's curse? The archaic confession in 1 Corinthians 15:3 shows where the answer was found: "Christ died for our sins according to the scriptures." The phrase "for our sins" implies that his death was a victorious one, while "according to the scriptures" backs this interpretation of Jesus' death with Isaiah 53—it is the only chapter in the Old Testament that contains a statement corresponding to "he died for our sins."

It will always remain difficult for me to understand how it could have been doubted that 1 Corinthians 15:3 alludes to Isaiah 53. At least no appeal should have been made to the plural "the scriptures." It has been argued that this plural cannot mean Isaiah 53 because it refers to a multitude of scriptural passages, not just one. This, however, is a philological error. The Greek plural "the scriptures" goes back to a similar Aramaic term that is just another expression for "the Bible," as "the Scriptures" is in English today. Besides, there are other proofs that the earliest churches applied Isaiah 53 to Jesus. Such references abound in Paul's writings. Now it is an impressive fact that not one of these was coined by Paul himself; all without exception are drawn from pre-Pauline tradition. This can be shown in some cases by style, in other cases by vocabulary, in most cases by both.[26] Thus it cannot reasonably be doubted that even in its earliest days the churches found in the chapter about the Suffering Servant the key to the dark riddle why the Son of God had to die under God's curse.

## Jesus' Interpretation of His Death

The Gospels report that this interpretation of Jesus' death goes back to Jesus himself. But can they be trusted?

One thing seems certain to me: the events during Jesus' ministry must have forced him to reckon more and more with the inevitability of his own persecution, and even a violent death. He had been reproached with transgression of the Sabbath, with blasphemy and with magic (Mark 3:22b). In each case the crime entailed the punishment of death by stoning (*m. Sanh.* 7.4), with subsequent hanging of the dead body (*m. Sanh.* 6.4). Furthermore, Jesus repeatedly reckoned himself among the prophets (such sayings stand a good chance of being authentic because of the seemingly modest Christology they imply). Now in his days, martyrdom was considered an integral part of the prophetic ministry; this fact is confirmed by the New Testament, the contemporary legends about the prophets, and the custom of honoring the prophets' tombs with monuments in expiation of their murder, a custom that came into vogue during Jesus' lifetime (Matt 23:29; Luke 11:47) and to which the great monuments of the Kidron Valley still bear witness today.[27] Jesus himself shared this view of the prophetic ministry and was convinced that the prophetic destiny awaited him also (Luke 13:33). He considered the history of salvation as an uninterrupted sequence of martyred saints from Abel to Zechariah, the son of Jehoiada (Matt 23:35), and he particularly took the fate of the last in the line, John the Baptist, as a hint of what awaited him (Mark 9:11-13).

Under these circumstances, we can only expect that Jesus spoke to his disciples about the fate he foresaw as the Gospels tell us. But here we must not overlook an important fact. For in speaking of Jesus' predictions of his passion, we usually think only of the direct announcements (Mark 8:31; 9:31; 10:33-34; and par.), which, by the way, are really three variants of one and the same announcement. But besides these plain and direct announcements, we have a great number of indirect announcements, which form the older and more important layer of tradition. I think that it has been a source of error that critical investigation has focused almost exclusively on the direct announcements. It is true that when we analyze these direct announcements of Jesus' passion along the lines of literary criticism we do observe a marked tendency of the Gospel tradition to put such statements into Jesus' mouth (Matt 26:2; see Mark 14:1) and in addition a tendency to assimilate such statements step by step to the historic course of events. These tendencies cannot be doubted, and it is easy to understand why many scholars have concluded from these that all of Jesus' announcements of his passion and resurrection that have come down to us are *vaticina ex eventu*—that they have all been created after the events they purport to predict. Actually, this conclusion is untenable. Even the most critical analysis of the direct announcements—leaving aside for the moment the indirect predictions—cannot but reveal a core in Jesus' sayings about his passion that must antedate the crucifixion.

Undoubtedly, the kernel of the direct announcements belongs to the pre-Hellenistic stratum of tradition. That is shown for instance by the play on words that appears when Mark 9:31 is retranslated into Aramaic: "God will surrender the man (*bar naša*)." It is also shown by the fact that these announcements almost never refer to the Greek text of the Old Testament but rather to the Hebrew text. Still weightier is the observation that the first of them (Mark 8:31) is so closely connected with its context, the rebuke of Peter, that it cannot be separated from it; this means that this announcement shares the claim to authenticity that must be attributed to Peter's designation as Satan in Mark 8:33.[28] Finally, this pre-Easter nucleus of the plain announcements becomes evident when we examine the phrase "after three days." At first glance, it seems probable that the sentence in Mark 8:31 (par.), "and after three days he will rise again," is entirely formulated *ex eventu*—after the events. But there are additional sayings referring to three days. After three days, Jesus affirms, he will build the new temple (Mark 14:58 and par.). He casts out demons and performs cures today and tomorrow, and the third day he will be perfected (Luke 13:32). A little while and they will see him no more; a little while later and they will see him again: today they have fellowship with him, tomorrow they will be separated, the third day the parousia will take place (John 16:16). It is quite clear that Jesus announced in various ways God's great triumph that was to change the world in three days—that is, after a short while. In all these "three days" sayings there is nowhere a distinction between the resurrection and the parousia. That, if nothing else, shows already that the substance of such announcements antedates Easter.

With these last remarks, we have already touched upon the indirect predictions of the passion, which are the more important ones, because they have not been submitted to a reshaping equal to that of the direct announcements.

These indirect announcements are very numerous and represent a broad variety of literary forms. There are similes (such as cup, baptism, ransom, the slain shepherd) and parables (such as the wicked tenants), riddle-sayings (so-called *mešalim*, like the one about Jonah or about the need of swords, as well as others), menacing sayings (such as Luke 13:32), the many announcements of the passion of the disciples, and the words of interpretation spoken at the Last Supper. This great variety shows that these indirect announcements are deeply rooted in the tradition. Even more significant is the fact that they contain a number of features that were not borne out literally by the subsequent events. For instance, Jesus seems to have thought it possible that he would be buried as a criminal (Mark 14:8), an indignity that was spared him, and that some of his disciples would have to share his fate (Mark 10:32-40; Luke 14:25-33; 22:36-37), which did not happen immediately; strangely enough, the authorities were content with executing Jesus and left his disciples alone.

Accumulated evidence of this kind forbids us to declare Jesus' announcements inauthentic in totality. Skepticism involuntarily turns into falsification of history if it allows itself to be carried away by individual critical observations, right as they may be, into attributing the whole of the material uncritically to the faith of the earliest churches.

Now if it be admitted that the substance of Jesus' announcements of his passion and of his glorification goes back to the Lord himself, then one has no right lightly to discard those passages that assert that Jesus not only announced but also interpreted his passion and to regard them as dogmas of the earliest churches. Quite the opposite! Whoever is even faintly familiar with the extraordinary importance the idea of the atoning power of suffering and death had attained in late Judaism will have to admit that it is completely inconceivable that Jesus would have expected to suffer and die without having reflected upon the meaning of these events.

Among the passages in question, first of all attention must be drawn to the Eucharistic words. What matters here are the words "for many." I will restrict myself to two remarks. In the first place, these words are preserved in all versions of the words of institution the New Testament hands down to us, although with some variations as to position and phrasing. Mark 14:24 reads "for many"; Matthew 26:28 reads "on behalf of many"; 1 Corinthians 11:24 and Luke 22:19-20 have "for you"; and finally, John 6:51 has "for the life of the world." Of the different versions of this expression, Mark's "for many," being a Semitism, is older than Paul's and Luke's "for you." Since Paul is likely to have received his formulation of the Eucharistic words in the beginning of the forties in Antioch,[29] Mark's "for many" leads us back into the first decade after Jesus' death. Whoever wishes to drop those two words as a secondary comment ought to realize that they are abandoning a very ancient piece of tradition and that there are no linguistic grounds on which they can stand. In the second place, the words "for many" are a reference to Isaiah 53, as Mark 10:45 confirms. The idea of substitution as well as the word "many" alludes to just this passage, for "many" without the article, in the inclusive sense of "the many," "the great number," "all," abounds in Isaiah 53 and constitutes something like the keyword of this chapter. Thus the phrase "for many" in the Eucharistic words shows that Jesus found the key to the meaning of his passion and death in Isaiah 53.[30]

A saying closely related to the Eucharistic words concerns ransom: Mark 10:45 (par. Matt 20:28). The history of its tradition is more complicated than that of the Eucharistic words, because Mark and Matthew differ from Luke 22:27. Mark and Matthew read: "For the Son of Man came not to be served but to serve, and to give his life a ransom for many." But Luke reads: "For who is the greater, the one who is at table or the one who serves? Is it not the one at the table? But I am among you as one who serves." What can be made of this seems to be that behind both versions there lies a saying in which Jesus spoke of himself as a servant. In the source peculiar to Luke, this service is illustrated by Jesus' waiting at table, in Mark by means of Isaiah 53. In Luke the context is strongly Hellenized as far as the language but also the imagery is Semitic, for the religious application of the simile of ransom is typically Palestinian. The least that must be said with regard to this saying is this: besides the Eucharistic words, Mark had one more piece of ancient tradition that presents Jesus as interpreting his passion with the aid of Isaiah 53.[31]

We meet another very old tradition in the saying about the swords (Luke 22:35-38), which comes from Luke's special source. I would venture to say that here we once more strike the bedrock of tradition. Jesus warns his disciples that the attitude of their compatriots toward them is going to shift abruptly from friendship and hospitality to fierce hatred. The peaceful times are past and gone. By all means, buy swords. The reason for this radical change is given by a quotation from Isaiah 53:12: "He was numbered with the transgressors." Jesus' passion will also mark the turning point of the fate of his followers. As soon as we realize that what Jesus announces is not just hatred and persecution but the immediately imminent beginning of the apocalyptic tribulation, it is evident that we are dealing with a saying that cannot have been coined after the events, but must be pre-Easter. In v. 38 there follows another very ancient saying, that of the disciples: "They said, 'Lord, look here are two swords.'" It must be ancient because it admits without concealing or glossing over the disciples' utter lack of understanding. Again it is Isaiah 53 that furnishes in Luke 22:35-38 the interpretation of the passion lying before Jesus.

No doubt we must also regard Mark 14:27-28, the saying about the shepherd who is slain and whose sheep are scattered, as belonging to pre-Easter tradition. The reason it must be so old lies in v. 28, where Jesus says: "But after I am raised up, I will go before you to Galilee." The decisive point is that "to go before" is shepherd language. That means that the promise that Jesus will go before his disciples to Galilee is still part of the simile of the shepherd. Now, the image of the shepherd preceding his flock and guiding them to Galilee can by no means have been worded after the resurrection. Rather, this image condenses Zechariah 13:7-9, where it says that the death of the shepherd ushers in not only the eschatological tribulation of the flock but also the gathering of the tried and purified remnant within the kingdom of God (see also Zech 14:9).[32] Again, as in Luke 22:35-38, it is Jesus' death that marks the turning point inaugurating the final tribulation and salvation. John 10, where the simile of the slain shepherd is taken up, stresses the vicarious significance of his death (10:11, 15) in terms reminiscent of Isaiah 53.

Finally, mention must be made of Luke 23:34, Jesus' intercession on the cross: "Father, forgive them; for they do not know what they are doing." This prayer is an addition to the oldest text but one that is based on ancient tradition, as both the form (God being addressed as Father, 'Abba') and the context (the intercession for enemies) show. Again we have in this prayer an implicit interpretation of Jesus' death. For Jesus offers it in place of the expiatory vow: "May my death expiate all my sins," which a condemned man had to say before his execution. Jesus applies the atoning virtue of his death not to himself, as was the custom, but to his executioners. Here again Isaiah 53 is in the background, closing with the words "and he made intercession for the transgressors" (Isa 53:12).

All five passages were of great importance for the earliest churches and were connected with their life: the words of institution with the Eucharist; the ransom-saying in Mark 10:45 with ethical instruction; Luke 23:34 with the life of prayer (see Acts 7:60); Luke 22:35-38 and Mark 14:27-28 with both handing down of the tradition about Jesus' passion and the churches' tribulations.

The number of instances where Jesus applies Isaiah 53 to himself is limited. The reason is that Jesus unveiled the deepest mysteries of his mission only to his disciples and not in his public teaching. Judaism in Jesus' time confirms this fact, showing us that the deepest meaning of the gathering of an inner circle of disciples was that they alone could share in the last insights of the master.[33] Thus Jesus let only his disciples share the secret that he considered the fulfillment of Isaiah 53 the task put before him by God; only to them did he interpret his death as a vicarious action in substitution for the "many," the countless number of those who were bound to be condemned by God. According to Isaiah 53, there are four reasons why the death of the Servant of God has such unlimited atoning power: his passion is voluntary (v. 10), patiently undergone (v. 7), in accordance with God's will (vv. 6, 10), and innocent (v. 9). It is life from God and with God that is here put to death.

If we have succeeded in tracing the earliest churches' interpretation of Jesus' death as a fulfillment of Isaiah back to Jesus himself with great probability—certainty is not to be expected at this point—we are still faced with the existential question whether all this is true, whether his death on Calvary was just one of the many martyrs' deaths that history records or whether it was the one vicarious death that atones for the sins of the world. This question remains. The answer to this decisive question, however, is entrusted not to the church, but to Jesus himself.

## JUSTIFICATION BY FAITH

### The Meaning of the Formula

I should like to lay the foundation for what follows by making some linguistic observations. We ask what is meant by: (1) to be justified, (2) by faith, (3) of grace?

Like the Hebrew verb *ṣadaq*, the Greek *dikaioun* in the LXX belongs to legal terminology.[34] In the active voice, it means "to do a person justice," "to declare a person innocent," "to acquit a defendant." Accordingly, the passive meaning is "to win in court," "to be declared innocent," "to be acquitted." In this sense, *dikaioun* is also used in the New Testament. Compare Matthew 12:37, a reference to the last judgment: "For by your words you will be acquitted (*dikaiōthēsē*), and by your words you will be condemned." The same contrast "to acquit" "to condemn" also occurs in Romans 8:33-34, a quotation from Isaiah 50:8: "It is God who acquits (*theos ho dikaiōn*). Who is to condemn?" All this can be read in any lexicon.

It must be noted, however, that the verb *dikaioun / dikaiousthai* had undergone an extension of its range of meaning, specifically when it was used of God's action. The new shade of meaning is first found in Deutero-Isaiah. Isaiah 45:25 reads in the LXX:

> From the Lord shall be justified (*dikaiōthēsetai*)
> and by God shall be glorified
> all the offspring of Israel.

In this saying Deutero-Isaiah clearly breaks through the bounds of the forensic usage. The parallelism between "to be justified" and "to be glorified" demonstrates that *dikaiousthai* here assumes the meaning "to find salvation."

As far as I know, it has not yet been noted that this usage lived on in postbiblical Judaism. At least two instances can be adduced. In Pseudo-Philo's

*Biblical Antiquities* (written after 70 C.E.) "to be justified" appears as a parallel to God's election (*Bib. Ant.* 49.4), and similarly in IV Ezra (written after 94 C.E.), "to find grace," "to be justified," and "to be heard in prayer" are used as synonyms (4 Ezra 12:7).

The last passage mentioned above is the beginning of a prayer. It reads:

> O most high Lord,
> if I have found grace in your eyes,
> and if I have been justified in your presence before many,
> and if my prayer assuredly rises to your countenance . . .

The last three lines are in parallelism. In the first and second of these "to find grace" alternates with "to be justified" without any apparent change of meaning. The literal translation "to be justified," therefore, is too narrow and does not get at the heart of the expression. Rather, what the text intends is:

> If I have found grace in your eyes,
> and if I have found good pleasure in your
> presence before many . . .

What is important here is that the idea of a trial in court has been abandoned. "To be justified" as applied to an act of God and paralleling "to find grace" does not have the narrow meaning of "to be acquitted," but rather the more extensive one, "to find good pleasure." This is confirmed by the third parallel line, which indicates how God's grace, his good pleasure, is expressed: it consists in God's hearing the prayer.

All this brings us within close reach of a saying from the Gospels, namely, Luke 18:14, where Jesus says concerning the tax collector: "I tell you, this man went down to his home justified rather than the other." Here too the forensic comparison is abandoned. Here too "to be justified" rather has the meaning "to find God's good pleasure." Here too this good pleasure of God manifests itself in that he hears prayer. Luke 18:14, then, has to be rendered accordingly: "I tell you, this man went down to his home as one whose prayer God had heard, and not the other."

We have thus encountered a use of *dikaiousthai* in which the forensic comparison seems to have been watered down or even completely abandoned. I should like to call this usage "soteriological" to distinguish it from the forensic usage.

It is obvious that in Paul, too, the use of "to justify" (or "to be justified") reaches far beyond the legal sphere. Even though the forensic aspect is by no means lacking—we have already mentioned the hymn-like ending of Romans 8 where Paul (in 8:33-34) uses the figure of the court trial in quoting Isaiah 50:8: "It is God who acquits (*dikaiōn*). Who is to condemn?"—the soteriological connotation governs his speech. For Paul, the active *dikaioun* means "to grant grace or good pleasure"; the passive *dikaiousthai* means "to find grace or good pleasure."

That the figure of court proceedings is absent becomes especially apparent where Paul talks about a justification that lies in the past, as, for instance, in Romans 4:2: "For if Abraham found grace (*edikaiōthē*) by works. . . ." Here in the story of Abraham's faith we are not dealing with a forensic scene but rather with a bestowing of God's grace. The same is true of Romans 5:1: "Therefore, since we have found grace (*dikaiōthentes*) by faith, we have peace with God"; and also in Romans 5:9: "Since we have found grace (*dikaiōthentes*) by his blood." God's justification is an outpouring of grace that far exceeds the legal sphere.

With regard to the substantive "God's righteousness" (*dikaiosynē . . . [tou] theou*), the soteriological connotation has been noted long ago, first, to my knowledge, by Ropes.[35] In the Psalms and in Deutero-Isaiah "Yahweh's righteousness" (*ṣidqat Yhwh*) is used alternately with God's salvation, God's mercy. This is precisely Paul's usage (with the exception of Romans 3:5, where, however, he is not speaking himself, but quoting an objection). Thus, for example, Romans 1:17 must not be rendered: "In the gospel the righteousness of God is revealed," but "In the gospel God's salvation is revealed."

In summary, as in the Pauline letters *dikaiōsynē (tou) theou* must be translated "God's salvation," so *dikaiousthai* must be rendered "to find God's grace."

Now we may turn to the words "by faith" (*pistis, ek pistis, dia pisteōs*). Whenever Paul speaks of God's salvation (*dikaiosynē*) and God's bestowing of his grace (*dikaioun*), he focuses attention entirely upon God. Everything is concentrated on the one vital question whether God is gracious or not, whether he grants his good pleasure or not, whether he says "Yes" to me or "No." When does God say "Yes"?

Paul answers: a person is justified, a person finds grace, through faith. Martin Luther, in his translation of Romans 3:28, has added one word. He says: "therefore we conclude that a person is justified by faith only" ("allein durch den Glauben"; *sola fide*). He has been criticized for this addition, but linguistically he was quite right. For it is a characteristic of the Semitic languages (and, for that matter, Paul's epistles time and again betray his Jewish background) that the word "only" or "alone" is usually left out even in places where Western usage would consider it indispensable. See, for example, Mark 9:41: "Whoever gives you a cup of water to drink because you bear the name of Christ will by no means lose the reward," where the sense is: "Whoever gives you *only* a cup of water; even this insignificant service will be rewarded." *Sola fide!* Faith is the only way to find God's grace.

When Paul speaks about finding grace by faith alone, it is always in contrast to finding grace by works. The doctrine of justification cannot be understood without this antithesis. It is directed against the basic conception of Judaism and Judaizing Christianity, according to which one finds God's grace by the fulfillment of the divine will. Paul also held this view up to the moment when Christ appeared to him on the way to Damascus. But this moment ended for him the illusion that one can stand up before God on one's own strength. And so, from Damascus on, he counters the thesis of the Judaizers, that the observance of the law is the way to salvation, with the antithesis: the way to God's grace is not by deeds; rather, it is by faith (Rom 3:28; 4:5; Gal 2:16; 3:8, 24).

Thus faith replaces works. But then the question arises: Are we again confronted with some achievement on the strength of which God is gracious if the justification follows because of faith? The answer here is: Yes! We are, in fact, confronted with an achievement. God does grant his grace on the basis of an achievement. But now it is not my achievement, but the achievement of Christ on the cross. Faith is not an achievement in itself; rather it is the hand that grasps the work of Christ and holds it out to God. Faith says: Here is the achievement—Christ died for me on the cross (Gal 2:20). This faith is the only way to obtain God's grace.

That God grants his good pleasure to the believer is against every rule of human law. This becomes clear when one considers who is justified: the ungodly (Rom 4:5), who deserve death because they bear the curse of God (Gal 3:10). God's good pleasure is granted to them "of grace" (Rom 4:5; 5:17), as a free gift (Rom 3:24). This grace knows of no restriction; being independent of the Mosaic law, it can also include the Gentiles. In Romans 4:6-8 we have in a nutshell what is implied by this finding God's good pleasure *sola gratia* ("by grace only"): David pronounces a blessing upon the one to whom God reckons righteousness apart from works:

> Blessed are those whose transgression is forgiven,
>     whose sin is covered;
> blessed are those to whom Yahweh
>     imputes no iniquity. (Ps 32:1-2a)[36]

Justification is forgiveness, nothing but forgiveness for Christ's sake. Yet this statement needs further clarification.

## Justification and New Creation

If we list the Pauline passages where the justification formula occurs, we come across an astonishing fact that is often overlooked, namely, that the doctrine of justification is missing altogether in most of the Pauline epistles. If we take the oldest of them, the two letters to the Thessalonians, we find no trace of it. In the first letter the adverb "righteous" (*dikaiōs*) indicates the blameless behavior of the apostle (1 Thess 2:10). In the second, God's judgment is called "righteous judgment"; God is called "just" because his judgment is impartial (2 Thess 1:5-6). These statements have nothing to do with the doctrine of justification. In Galatians, which is the next letter chronologically, the full formula "justification by faith" or "to be justified by faith" suddenly appears for the first time. In the two letters to the Corinthians, *dikaiosynē* has the meaning "salvation," and "to be justified" occurs at least once (1 Cor 6:11) in the specifically Pauline sense. But nowhere does the full formula of "justification by faith" appear in either letter. We then find the full formula most frequently in Romans. But again, it is missing in the Prison Epistles (Philippians, Ephesians, Colossians, Philemon), except in Philippians 3:9, where salvation (*dikaiosynē*) by law is set over against the salvation (*dikaiosynē*) of God by faith. The Pastoral Epistles do not contain the full formula, though Titus 3:7 uses the following variation: "justified by his grace." Thus, the full formula "justification by faith" or "to be justified by faith" is limited to three epistles: Galatians, Romans, and Philippians (and in the last to one verse only); we may also add Titus 3:7. This is a very striking fact. How is it to be explained?

The answer is the doctrine occurs exclusively where Paul is engaged in debate with Judaism. Certainly William Wrede was right when he concluded that the doctrine of justification was a polemic doctrine arising out of the dispute with Judaism and its nomistic theology.[37] But Wrede went even further; and, from the limited occurrence of the formula, he concluded that the doctrine of justification does not stand in the center of Pauline theology. Albert Schweitzer seconded him with the now famous formulation according to which the doctrine of justification is but a "subsidiary crater, which has formed within the rim of the main crater" of Paul's mystical experience of life in Christ.[38] Is this a correct conclusion? I think not. Both Wrede and Schweitzer are mistaken in their failure to ask one question, namely: How is justification bestowed? How does God accept the ungodly? In this matter we see things more clearly today because we have learned in the last decades that it is in baptism that this bestowal takes place. This follows, for example, from 1 Corinthians 6:11, where the verb "to be justified" is surrounded by baptismal terms and formulas: "But you were washed, you were sanctified, you were justified in the name of the Lord Jesus Christ and in the Spirit of our God" (see also Rom 6:7; Gal 3:24-27; Tit 3:5-7). Paul does not stress explicitly the connection between justification and baptism for the very simple reason that in the justification formula the term "by faith" includes baptism by way of abbreviation, as Rudolf Schnackenburg has convincingly shown.[39] The connection of justification with baptism is so obvious to Paul that he feels no necessity to state in so many words that it is in baptism that God saves those who believe in Jesus Christ.

Here we must remind ourselves that Paul speaks and writes as a missionary. In the missionary situation, for the Gentile or the Jew who believed in the good news and decided to join the Christian congregation, baptism was the decisive act for inclusion among those belonging to Jesus as their Lord. Therefore, Paul incessantly stresses the importance of baptism, and he uses a multitude of illustrations to show to the newly converted what this rite means to them. As one might summarize what he tells them: When you are baptized you are washed; you are cleansed; you are sanctified; you are buried in the water and by this burial you get a share in Christ's death and resurrection; you are putting on Christ like a garment; you are incorporated into his body; you are adopted and you become sons of God; you are circumcised with the circumcision made without hands, that is, you are made members of God's people; in short, you are included in the kingdom.

The formula "justification by faith" is but one of these manifold illustrations. It is the description of God's grace in baptism using a figure taken originally from the judicial sphere: God's grace in baptism consists in his undeserved pardon. It is that formulation of the grace of baptism that Paul created in conflict with Judaism. Therefore it is not a "subsidiary crater," but it occupies a place of equal importance with all the other descriptions of the grace of baptism. See again 1 Corinthians 6:11: "But you were washed, you were sanctified, you were justified in the name of the Lord Jesus Christ and in the Spirit of our God."

This statement has a far-reaching consequence, namely, that the doctrine of justification should not be isolated. On the contrary, it can only be understood in connection with all the other pronouncements about baptism. God's grace through baptism is so comprehensive that each of the many illustrations, images, and comparisons that Paul uses expresses only one aspect of it. If he speaks of ablution, the stress is upon deliverance from the uncleanness of the old existence. If he uses the image of the putting on of Christ, borrowed from the language of mysticism, the emphasis is upon communion, even unity, with the risen Lord. The same intention, with the additional connotation of the unity of Christians with one another, is expressed by the image of incorporation into the body of Christ. If he uses the expression "the circumcision of Christ" the point is inclusion in the new people of God. Finally, if he adopts the originally forensic language of justification, he intends to say that God alone is at work. Man does nothing; God does all.

Once again, no single image can exhaust the boundless wealth of God's grace. Rather, each is but a "part for the whole" (*pars pro toto*) description that stands for the whole gift. To isolate the forensic image, therefore, could lead to a misunderstanding. It would lie in the conclusion that the grace of God given in baptism is merely forensic, that we are dealing with a mere "as if": God acquits the ungodly and treats him as if he were righteous.

This came out very clearly in an interesting controversy between Rudolf Bultmann and Hans Windisch in 1924, at a time when dialectic theology was enjoying its vogue. Bultmann wrote on "The Problem of Ethics in Paul."[40] His subject was the problem of the apparent contradiction between indicative and imperative, that is the paradoxical antinomy that we find for instance in 1 Corinthians 5:7: "Clean out the old yeast so that you may be a new batch, as you really are unleavened." Or in Galatians 5:25: "If we live by the Spirit, let us also be guided by the Spirit." Bultmann rejected most emphatically and convincingly previous attempts at a merely psychological solution of this problem. In contrast, he stressed the eschatological character of divine justification. He insisted rightly that justification is not a change in the moral qualities of people, that it is not an experience akin to mystical experiences, that it can only be believed in. But I think he was misled when he added that the continuity of the old and the new person is not interrupted, that the believer does not cease to be ungodly and that he is always justified only as an ungodly person. Bultmann himself admitted freely that Paul does not say this. But he maintained that Paul had not pressed his thinking to its own conclusions and that the modern interpretation must make explicit what Paul omitted.

Windisch contradicted Bultmann in the same year (1924) in an article titled "The Problem of the Pauline Imperative."[41] Windisch was an exponent of the old liberal school, and several of his assertions clearly betray this. But he recognized the weak point in Bultmann's view. He remarked ironically that evidently Paul urgently needed to listen to a lecture by Karl Barth or perhaps Rudolf Bultmann.[42] Against Bultmann he insisted that according to the apostle the continuity between the old and the new is completely broken, as radically as by death and resurrection—"So if anyone is in Christ, there is a new creation" (2 Cor 5:17a). Briefly stated, the spirit (*pneuma*) is a reality that takes possession of the baptized and breaks the continuity between the old and the new existence.

This controversy is instructive insofar as the position of Bultmann (which, by the way, he did not maintain in his *Theology of the New Testament*)[43] shows how dangerous it is to isolate the doctrine of justification. If we contend that the believer does not cease to be ungodly and if justification consists merely in a change of God's judgment, then we come dangerously close to the misunderstanding that justification is only an "as if." This surely was not Paul's intention. We have seen that for him justification was only one of the many attempts to describe the inexhaustible and unutterable riches of God's grace and that we must include justification in all the other sayings interpreting baptism in order to put it in its proper setting.

Now the common denominator of all sayings on baptism is that they describe God's gracious action as resulting in a new creation (2 Cor 5:17a). And this new creation, Paul continues, has two sides: "Everything old has passed away; see, everything has become new!" (2 Cor 5:17b). The old existence has come to an end; sin is washed away; the domination of the flesh and of the dark powers, including law, is broken. A new life begins: the gift of God's Spirit is granted and is manifested as an effective power. Those incorporated in Christ do not remain what they were. Christ is their life (Col 3:4); Christ is their peace (Eph 2:14). We always find these two aspects: God has delivered us from the power of darkness and has transferred us into the kingdom of his dear son (Col 1:13).

This is also true of justification. Although it is quite certain that justification is and remains a forensic action (God's amnesty), nevertheless, the forensic image is shattered. God's acquittal is not only forensic, it is not an "as if," not a mere word; but it is God's word that works and creates life. God's word is always an effective word. The forgiveness, the good pleasure that God grants, is not only negative—an effacement of the past—but it is an antedonation of God's final gift. (The word "anticipation," which one might expect to be used here, is an unfortunate expression because it is derived from the Latin *anticipere*, meaning "to take in advance." The sense at this point seems much better served by the word *antedonation*, which means a "donation made in advance.") As an antedonation of God's final acquittal, justification is pardon in the fullest sense. It is the beginning of a new life, a new existence, a new creation through the gift of the Holy Spirit. As Luther put it: "Where remission of sin is, there is life and salvation."[44]

The new life in Christ, given in baptism, is renewed again and again in the Eucharist. It is true that the verb "to be justified" does not appear when Paul speaks about the Lord's Supper. But this is not astonishing when one considers that Paul, by chance, deals with the Eucharist at length only in 1 Corinthians 10 and 11, both of which are concerned with practical questions: the sacrifice offered to idols and the sharing of the meal with the poor brethren. Both of these sections, especially 1 Corinthians 10:16, show that Paul understood the Eucharist to convey the same gift as baptism: a sharing in Christ's vicarious death and in the communion of his body. Thus the Eucharist renews

God's grace given in baptism for which justification is but one of the many descriptions.

As an antedonation of God's final salvation, justification points to the future. It shares the double nature of all gifts of God: they are present possessions and yet objects of hope. Justification is a firm present possession (Rom 5:1 et al.) and nevertheless it lies at the same time in the future, as emphasized, for example, in Galatians 5:5: "For through the Spirit, by faith, we eagerly wait for the hope of salvation (*dikaiosynē*)." Justification, then, is the beginning of a movement toward a goal, namely, toward the hour of the definitive justification, of the acquittal on the day of judgment, when the full gift is realized.

For this reason, God's justification of the sinner is no dead possession; rather, it imposes an obligation. God's gift can be lost. The justified still stands in the fear of God. Justification takes place in the tension between possession and hope. But it is hope grounded on a firm foundation. In Romans 5:8-9 we read: "But God proves his love for us in that while we still were sinners Christ died for us. Much more surely then, now that we have been justified by his blood, will we be saved through him from the wrath of God." This is not a conclusion "from the lesser to the greater" (*a minori ad maius*) but "from the greater to the lesser" (*a maiori ad minus*). God has done the greater thing: Christ died for us while we were still sinners—how much more, being justified, can we be certain that he will grant us the final salvation.

To sum up, it remains true that justification is forgiveness, nothing but forgiveness. But justification is forgiveness in its fullest sense. It is not only a mere covering up of the past. Rather, it is an antedonation of the full salvation; it is a new creation by God's Spirit; it is Christ taking possession of the life already now, already here.

### The Origin of the Pauline Doctrine of Justification

Is Paul's doctrine of justification entirely new? Or does it have an older root? Is this doctrine that God gives his good pleasure to the ungodly because of his faith, purely by grace, to be found earlier than Paul?

It has recently been maintained that the Qumran texts anticipate what Paul had to say about justification.[45] Reference has been made primarily to the surprising similarity to Paul allegedly displayed by the concluding psalm in the Community Rule (1QS 11.2-22). It has been held that this passage attests the presence of the doctrine of justification by grace alone (*sola gratia*) in Qumran. The text has been translated as follows:

> But as for me, my justification (*mišpaṭi*) belongs to God,
> and in his hand is the blamelessness of my conduct,
> together with the uprightness of my heart,

> and in his righteousness my transgression will be wiped
>   out. (1QS 11.2-3)

> For the source of his righteousness comes my
>   justification (*mišpaṭi*),
> a light in my heart from his marvelous mysteries. (11.5)

> If I stumble in sinful flesh,
> my justification (*mišpaṭi*) will remain eternally
> through God's righteousness (11.12)

> Through his mercies he let me approach,
> and through his gracious manifestation comes my
>   justification (*mišpaṭi*);
> by the justice of his truth he has justified me (*šephaṭani*)
> and in his great kindness he will atone for all my sins,
> and by his justice he will cleanse me from all human
>   uncleanness. (11.13-14)

Does this text warrant the conclusion that has been drawn from it? The interpretation of the lines quoted above hinges upon the word *mišpaṭi*, which has been rendered "justification" in this translation. But this translation is not correct. For neither in the Old Testament nor in the literature of late Judaism does *mišpaṭi* designate anywhere the justification of the ungodly, nor does *šephaṭani* mean to justify the ungodly. The translation cited above, current though it may be, does not accurately convey the intention of the text. Rather, careful attention to the words used in parallelism with *mišpaṭi* shows that *mišpaṭi* is God's gracious decision over the path of the life of the one praying.[46] This decision is realized in God's letting the supplicant "approach" (a technical term for entrance into the community) and thereby making possible for the supplicant the "blameless conduct" in perfect obedience to the Torah, a conduct humans are not able to achieve alone. If one stumbles on this path, God wipes out one's sins and maintains his decision, provided the heart of the supplicant is sincere. Thus *mišpaṭi* is not the justification of the ungodly (*justificatio impii*), but rather predestination to the path of perfect obedience to the Torah.

A particularly instructive example of how inadmissible it is to put Paul and Qumran on the same level is furnished by the interpretation the Habakkuk Commentary (1QpHab) gives to Habakkuk 2:4, the central proof text for the Pauline doctrine of justification: "The righteous shall live by his faith." 1QpHab 8.1-3 reads: "The interpretation (of this verse) concerns all the doers of the law in the house of Judah (and) those whom God will rescue from the house of judgment (that is, the last judgment) because of their labor and their loyalty toward the Teacher of Righteousness."

Qumran says, God will save the one who fulfills the law, faithfully following the Torah as interpreted by the Teacher. Paul interprets Habakkuk 2:4 quite differently: God grants life to the ungodly person who renounces all self-achievement and believes in Jesus Christ.

No! Qumran is not preliminary to Paul. Qumran is indeed aware of God's goodness and God's forgiveness, but they are valid only for those who attempt to fulfill the law to the last ounce of their strength. To sum up, Qumran and Paul belong to two different worlds: Qumran stands completely in the line of the law; Paul stands in the line of the good news.

But if Qumran does not represent a preliminary stage to the Pauline doctrine of justification, we do in fact find a prefiguration at one other point; we do find the teaching that the keeping of the law and pious achievements do not count with God, that he does not want to deal with the righteous but with the sinner. One other person before Paul said this: Jesus.

It is the message of Jesus concerning the God who wants to deal with sinners that Paul takes up and expounds in his doctrine of justification by faith. This message, unique and unprecedented, was the center of Jesus' preaching. This is shown by all those parables in which God embraces those who are lost and reveals himself as the god of the poor and needy, as well as by Jesus' table-fellowship with tax collectors and sinners. The fact that Paul takes up this message of Jesus is easily overshadowed if one confines oneself to the concordance. It is true that many of the most important terms used by Paul, such as faith, grace, church, occur in only a few places in the sayings of Jesus. Nevertheless, the substance of all these terms is present there. For example, Jesus usually does not say church (*ekklēsia*), but he speaks of the flock of God, the family of God, the vineyard of God. Paul constantly translates into theological vocabulary what Jesus had expressed in images and parables taken from everyday life.

This is also to the point regarding the doctrine of justification. The doctrine is nothing else but Jesus' message of the God who wants to deal with the sinners, expressed in theological terms. Jesus says, "I have come to call not the righteous but sinners to repentance" (Luke 5:32); Paul says God "justifies the ungodly" (Rom 4:5). Jesus says, "Blessed are the poor" (Luke 6:20); Paul says we "are justified by his grace" (Rom 3:24). Jesus says, "Leave the dead to bury their own dead" (Luke 9:60; a powerful word that implies that outside the kingdom one finds nothing but death); Paul says, "The one who is justified by faith will have life." The vocabulary is different but the content is the same.

According to Luke, Jesus occasionally even used the forensic terminology of justification to describe God's bestowing of his good pleasure upon the lost.

Earlier I quoted Luke 18:14: "I tell you, this man went down to his home justi-fied rather than the other." And we have seen that the meaning is as follows: "I tell you, this man went home having found God's good pleasure, and not the other." At this point Luke cannot be dependent on Paul on linguistic grounds, for he uses a non-Greek idiomatic Semitism avoided by Paul.[47] We must con-clude, then, that not only the content of the Pauline doctrine of justification but also the terminology of an antedonated eschatological pardon goes back to Jesus.

Paul's greatness was that he understood the message of Jesus as no other New Testament writer did. He was the faithful interpreter of Jesus. This is especially true of his doctrine of justification. It is not of his own making, but in its substance, it conveys the central message of Jesus as it is condensed in the first beatitude, "Blessed are you who are poor, for yours is the kingdom of God" (Luke 6:20).

# The Revealing Word

## *The Literary Form of the Johannine Prologue*

As the beginning of a book, the Prologue to the Gospel of John is a unique pas-sage. The usual opening of a book can be observed in the other five books of the New Testament, as well as the twenty-one epistles. Here we find two forms employed. The first one is represented, for instance, by Revelation 1:1: "The revelation of Jesus Christ, which God gave him to show his servants what must soon take place; he made it known by sending his angel to his servant John." The opening passage here is a summary of the contents of the whole book. The preface to the Gospel of Luke is similar. In it we are told about preceding investigations, sources, and the intention and special character of the book. In the same way, Luke prefaced the second volume of his work, the Acts of the Apostles, with a summary of his first volume. The other usual way of begin-ning a book is employed in Matthew 1:1: "An account of the genealogy of Jesus the Messiah, the son of David, the son of Abraham"; and probably in Mark, which could, or rather should, be translated: "How Jesus Christ, the Son of God, began to announce the good news." Here, in each case, the opening con-sists in the heading of the first chapter. In other words, a book is ordinarily begun either with a preface to the whole work or with the heading of its first chapter.

The Gospel of John is quite different, confronting us with the enigmatic opening: "In the beginning was the Word." In order to understand this peculi-arity, we must direct our attention to the literary form of John 1:1-18. Three observations may be in order.

The first observation concerns sentence structure. The prologue is constructed by means of parallelism, the pairing of similarly sounding clauses, constituting a kind of call and response—perhaps echoing the alternation between presenter and congregation. We are familiar with this literary form from the Psalms. In the Near East, parallelism has the same function as the use of rhyme in our languages: together with meter, it distinguishes poetry from prose.[48] In other words, John 1:1-18 is a poetic passage. The prologue, as everyone knows today, is a powerfully contrived song, an early Christian religious poem, a psalm, a hymn to the Logos Jesus Christ.

The Logos-hymn divides itself naturally into four strophes:

> 1. The Logos of God (vv. 1-5)
> 2. The witness pointing to him (vv. 6-8)
> 3. The fate of the Logos in the world (vv. 9-13)
> 4. The confession of the believing community (vv. 14-18)

Three forms of parallelism are commonly used: synonymous (the second line repeating the content of the first); antithetic (the second line saying the opposite of the first); and synthetic (the second line adding a new idea to the first).[49] But in the Johannine Prologue we find a very pronounced and seldom used fourth kind: a skillful elaboration of the synthetic form, namely climactic parallelism (step parallelism). It is so named because every line takes up a word of the preceding line, as if it were lifting it up a step higher. In the Synoptic Gospels we find an example of this form in Mark 9:37 (and par.):

> Whoever receives one such child in my name
>> receives me;
> and whoever receives me,
> receives not me but him who sent me.

In the Johannine Prologue, it is represented, for instance, in vv. 4-5 and vv. 14b and 16 (leaving out v. 15 for reasons that will be mentioned presently):

> In him was *life,*
>> and the *life* was the *light* of all people.
> The *light* shines in the *darkness,*
>> and the *darkness* did not overcome it.
> We have beheld his *glory,*
>> *glory* as of a father's only son,
>> *full* of *grace* and truth.
> From his *fullness* have we all received, *grace* upon *grace.*
>> (au. trans., italics added)

This climactic parallelism is the dominating formal feature of the prologue. It is, however, lacking in some verses. We observed already that in vv. 14-16 we could only obtain a climactic parallelism by the catchword "full of grace" that connects v. 14b with v. 16, omitting v. 15. Similarly, vv. 12b and 13 also are devoid of climactic parallelism. This observation corresponds to another one. Whereas the climactic parts of the prologue differ in their vocabulary from the Fourth Gospel (such important words as "the Logos," "grace and truth," even "grace," do not recur outside the prologue), the nonclimactic insertions betray the language of the Fourth Evangelist himself (vv. 6-8, 12b-13, 15, and perhaps 17-18). It has, therefore, rightly been concluded and commonly accepted that we have to distinguish in the Johannine Prologue between the original prologue (almost certainly composed in Greek) and the comments of the Evangelist about it. In the same manner we find quoted in Philippians 2:6-11 a pre-Pauline Christ-hymn, in which Paul has inserted comments. Rudolf Bultmann maintained that the original prologue came from the circle of the followers of John the Baptist, but this is refuted by Luke 1, which shows that the disciples of the Baptist spoke of the miraculous signs at his birth but did not ascribe pre-existence to their master. This means that the original prologue must be of Christian origin. It was one of the hymns sung at the daily Eucharist *Christo quasi Deo* ("to Christ as to God"), as Pliny puts it in his famous letter to Trajan (*Ep.* 10.96).

Now we can go a step further. The Logos-hymn is one of the many in the New Testament. Like all mission churches and all vital communities, the early church was a singing church. The flow of new life and the surging of great spiritual energy in the church naturally was felt again and again in song, hymn, and praise. Psalms were on every lip. "Let the word of Christ dwell in you richly, as you teach and admonish one another in all wisdom, and as you sing psalms and hymns and spiritual songs with thankfulness in your hearts to God" (Col 3:16; par. Eph 5:19). The services of the early church were one continual jubilation, one great concord of worship and praise.

In this rejoicing, in these hymns, we find a wealth of different themes. It is hardly by chance that we find the greatest number of hymns and doxologies in the Book of Revelation. Here the dominating themes are the praise of God, the eternal King, and of the Lamb together with the thanksgiving for deliverance. The persecuted church is always one step ahead, and amid tribulation it anticipates in its hymns the final consummation. In the same manner, the final salvation is anticipated in the two hymns in Luke 1: the *Magnificat* (1:46-55) and the *Benedictus* (1:68-79). Romans 11:33-36 extols God's inscrutable ways, 1 Corinthians 13 praises love. Other psalms exalt Christ: Phil 2:6-11; Col 1:15-20; 1 Tim 3:16; 2 Tim 2:11-13.

Of all these New Testament hymns, the one undoubtedly most akin to the Christ-hymn in John 1 is Philippians 2:6-11. Not only are both songs about

Christ, not only would Pliny's phrase *Christ quasi Deo* apply to each of them (see Phil 2:6 and John 1:1), but they also differ from all the other hymns in the New Testament in that they relate, narrate, and preach the story of Christ.[50] They are "salvation history" (*Heilsgeschichte*) in hymnic form. This literary genre, in which the history of salvation is chanted in psalmodic form, comes from the Old Testament; we need only compare the psalms extolling God's guidance of his people throughout their history, for example Psalm 78.

Two examples from the second century C.E., taken from different, even opposite realms, may show the development of this literary genre in the early church and illustrate it at the same time. The first is the second article of the Creed, which tells and confesses in hymnic praise the story of Jesus Christ to the time of the parousia. The second example is the so-called Naassene Hymn, transmitted by Hippolytus in his book *Refutation of All Heresies*. It begins by naming the three principles underlying all that exists, then gives a dramatic account of how the soul, like a timid deer, is hunted by death and is unable to find any escape from the labyrinth, and how Jesus offers to save it.

> The world's producing law was Primal Mind,
> and next was First-born's outpoured Chaos;
> and third, the soul received its law of toil:
> encircl'd, therefore, with an aqueous form,
> with care o'erpowered it succumbs to death.
> Now holding sway, it eyes the light,
> and now it weeps on misery flung;
> now it mourns, now it thrills with joy;
> now it wails, now it hears its doom;
> now it hears its doom, now it dies,
> and now it leaves us, never to return.
> It, hapless straying, treads the maze of ills.
> But Jesus said, Father, behold
> a strife of ills across the earth
> wanders from thy breath [of wrath];
> but bitter Chaos [man] seeks to shun,
> and knows not how to pass it through.
> Bearing seals I shall descend;
> through ages whole I'll sweep,
> all mysteries I'll unravel,
> and forms of Gods I'll show;
> and secrets of the saintly path,
> styled "Gnosis," I'll impart. (*Ref.* 5.5)[51]

What we have here is a Christ-hymn that begins, like the Johannine Prologue, with primordial origins and then tells about the pre-existent Christ and
his compassion. Again we are confronted with "salvation history" in hymnic
form. And yet the Naassene Hymn, on the one hand, and Philippians 2, John 1,
and the Creed, on the other hand, belong to two entirely different worlds:
Gnostic Christianity and the gospel. To characterize these worlds bluntly:
Gnosticism affirms that the greatest of all evils is death, but the gospel affirms
that the greatest of all evils is sin. Gnosticism asserts that the way of salvation
is revealed knowledge (*gnōsis*), but the gospel asserts that the way of salvation
is pardon for our sins.[52]

Nevertheless, we must take a final step. At one point in the hymn, there is a
break, an interruption. The first three strophes (John 1:1-13) are cast in the
third person. The last strophe (1:14-18), it is true, starts in the same way ("The
word became flesh") but immediately changes to the first person: "We have
beheld his glory, we have received grace upon grace." That means that the
Christ-hymn ends in a personal confession; it reaches its climax in thanks,
praise, and adoration. There can be no doubt that it is not the opening part,
the first three strophes, that contains the real substance of the psalm, but
rather the confession of faith in the last strophe. Everything that comes before
is only an introduction, a prelude, which serves to prepare for this confession.
The prologue is not primarily a dogmatic passage presenting us with christological speculations about Christ's pre-existence, his part in the creation of
the world, and his incarnation—to take it so would be a grave misunderstanding. Rather, it is the hymnal exaltation, by the believing community, of
God's unspeakable gift through him in whom God's glory has been revealed.

Why did the evangelist place this hymn to Christ at the beginning? Is it, as
has been held, a summary of his Gospel? If so, the passion and the resurrection should have been explicitly mentioned. The right answer is to be drawn
from the context. The story of John the Baptist follows in 1:19-36. This shows
that the prologue stands in the position that is occupied in Matthew and Luke
by the birth and infancy narratives. The fourth evangelist has no account of
the nativity but rather replaces the Christmas story with the Logos psalm. The
community of faith, so to speak, can no longer be satisfied with the prose version of the incarnation; it falls on its knees and worships with a hymn of
praise: "We have seen it, we have experienced it, we have beheld his glory."

We now have the answer to our question, how the strange beginning of the
Gospel of John is to be explained. The evangelist begins his book on an exalted
note. Apparently he has the feeling that the articulation of the gospel is
incompatible with the usual sober pattern of the beginning of a book. He
starts, therefore, with the powerful Logos hymn, teaching us that the proclamation of the gospel can never strike too high a note.

## The Train of Thought

THE FIRST STROPHE (1:1-5). In the first strophe, the Logos is presented in a threefold manner.

"In the beginning was the Word." The Logos-hymn starts with an intentional reminiscence of the first words of the Bible: "In the beginning God created the heavens and the earth" (Gen 1:1). But the word "beginning" has a different meaning in the prologue from what it has in Genesis. It does not designate the creation (which is mentioned only later, in John 1:3), but eternity before all creation. In other words, "In the beginning" in John 1:1 is not a temporal concept, but a qualitative one, equivalent to the sphere of God. The Logos has its origin in eternity; those who deal with the Logos have to deal with the living God himself.

Then the Logos is presented as the mediator in creation. "All things were made through him, and without him was not anything made that was made."[53] What is the meaning of this theological statement (*theologoumenon*)? Verse 10 gives the answer. "He was in the world, and although the world was made by him, it did not recognize him." That the world was made through him is the ground for the claim of Jesus Christ to sovereign authority over all. Thus, v. 3, "all things were made by him," says: all people stand under the claim of the Logos—everyone, whether they acknowledge this or not.

Finally, this Logos was the light of people. "In him was life, and the life was the light of people." That the Logos was the light of people has often been misunderstood in that it was thought to mean that the Logos imparted the inner light—the light of reason and of insight—to all human beings. Clearly this is not the meaning. As the following sentence ("the darkness has not comprehended it") shows, this light is not of this world. Rather, this light is the light of the new creation, the eschatological light, with its strange double effect of making the blind see and the seeing blind (John 9:39). This saving light shone in the darkness, but it shone in vain—"the darkness has not comprehended it." People loved the darkness more than the light.

THE SECOND STROPHE (1:6-8). Before the evangelist continues his quotation of the hymn, he inserts a short passage of his own that tells how God announced the coming of the Logos through a prophet called John. The Baptist is honored as the God-sent witness to Christ, but any overestimation of him is sharply repudiated. "He was not the light" (v. 8). This statement must have been of great concern to the evangelist because he stresses it again in v. 15, another of his insertions: the Baptist witnessed to Christ as being superior to himself because Christ came from eternity. The reason for this warning not to overestimate the Baptist may be found in the situation of the church in Asia Minor at the end of the first century C.E.: Acts 19 suggests that there was a rivalry at Ephesus between the followers of the Baptist and the church. But the reason could also be a personal one: perhaps the speaker here is someone who himself once had thought of the Baptist as the light until he met Jesus.

THE THIRD STROPHE (1:9-13). Now the hymn goes on telling us more about the fate of the Logos in the world. "The true light that 'lights' every person was coming into the world" (v. 9). It is important to understand the clause "that 'lights' every person" correctly. It has often been interpreted to mean, "that enlightens every human being." But this Platonic understanding of the light as an inner light shared by all human beings is in contradiction to v. 5 (see the analysis of the first strophe) as well as to vv. 7-8. Rather, "To light" signifies "to throw light upon, to reveal," and it is exactly in this way that John 1:9 is interpreted in 3:19-21. Thus the sentence "the true light that 'lights' every person was coming into the world" says that the eschatological light that shone into the darkness had an all-revealing power. With an unavoidable clarity that could not be deceived, it brought out the state of humanity before God. This revealing power of the Logos was the reason why the world "did not know him" (v. 10), which does not mean that the world did not recognize him because he was disguised, but rather (in an Old Testament usage of "to know") that the world denied him and refused to obey him. Even among "his own," in Israel, he stood before closed doors, a stranger even on his own estate (v. 11). Such was the fate of the Logos in the world.

Yet not everywhere. There were some who received him; and where he was admitted, where people believed in him, there he brought a gift above all gifts: "to them he gave power to become children of God" (v. 12a). What it means "to become a child of God" is explained by the evangelist in an additional remark that makes use of a fundamental notion of Johannine theology: dualism. Again and again the Fourth Gospel repeats that there are two kinds of life, two possibilities of existence: life from below and life from above, flesh and spirit, natural life and life through rebirth, earthly sonship and divine sonship.[54] This dualism is used in v. 13 to clarify the gift of the Logos, "to become children of God." Natural birth, though not to be despised in itself, does not enable one to see God as God is. There is only one way to God: rebirth, and there is only one who can give it: the Logos.

THE FOURTH STROPHE (vv. 14-18). The story of the Logos reaches its climax with the confession of the believing community. It begins, "And the Word became flesh and dwelt among us" (v. 14a). In our era we can hardly imagine how scandalous, and even blasphemous, this sentence must have sounded to John's contemporaries. It contained two offenses. The first is the word "flesh." "Flesh" describes humans in contrast to God by pointing to their frailty and mortality; it is the strongest expression of contempt for human existence. To say "the eternal Logos became flesh" is to say that he appeared in profound abasement. Even more offensive must have been the words "and dwelt among us." For "to dwell," "to tabernacle," is a biblical metaphor for God's presence (see, for example, Mark 9:5; Luke 16:9; Rev 7:15; 21:3). He "dwelt among us" implies that God himself was present in the flesh, in abasement. Here the decisive question arises: How can one say this? How can one say of a man who felt hunger and thirst, who knew fear and trembling, who died as a criminal, that God was present in him?

The answer is a simple confession consisting of two clauses. The first states: "We have seen his glory." The Greek text uses a verb here (*theasthai*) that has a special meaning. Like the usual word for "to see" (*horan*) in the Fourth Gospel, it always denotes a real seeing with physical eyes; but unlike *horan*, it can designate a seeing that penetrates beneath the surface. Thus "we beheld his glory" means: We have seen the flesh, the lowliness of shame, the deep disgrace of the cross; but behind this veil of flesh and humiliation, we beheld the glory of God.

What does "the glory of God" mean? The answer is given by the twofold phrase "full of grace and truth." This is Old Testament covenant language. "Grace and truth" summarizes what the faithful experienced in the covenant: "Yahweh, Yahweh, a God merciful and gracious, slow to anger, and abounding in grace and truth" (Exod 34:6). "I am not worthy of the least of all the mercies and of all the truth that you have shown to your servant" (Gen 32:10). In the covenant, the pious of the Old Testament had a double experience. They experienced God's mercy, of which they were unworthy, and more than this, God's truth, his constancy in this mercy. "Grace and truth" describe the steadfastness of divine mercy. This was precisely the glory that became visible in Jesus. Those who belonged to him encountered in him the constancy of God's faithfulness. In everything that he did and said, one and the same thing always emerged, "grace and truth," an unchanging divine mercy.

But the testimony of the community goes beyond the confession "we have beheld his glory, full of grace and truth," to include this statement as well: "And from his fullness have we all received grace upon grace" (v. 16). We have not only beheld his unchanging grace, but we have received it. The expression "grace upon grace" describes an endless progression and intensification. Out of an inexhaustible well we received one gift of God after another, each gift being greater than the preceding one. Such was the disciples' experience of Jesus. This is the whole answer of the believing community to the question: How can you say that in the man Jesus the eternal God dwelt among us? The answer is provided by pointing to his glory, the constancy of God's mercy and grace: we beheld it and we received it.

Here ends the story of the Logos, but not the prologue. Rather, as a kind of summary, two antitheses are added that conclude the hymn by emphasizing the significance of the revelation in Christ. This revelation is first of all contrasted with that of the Old Testament. "The law was given through Moses; grace and truth came through Jesus Christ" (v. 17). Once before God had given to people a great gift, his law, his holy will. But this was only the preparatory revelation. Now, in Jesus, God has really revealed himself and the fullness of his unchanging grace. Above the law stands grace.

The second and final antithesis goes even further. Most boldly, it contrasts the revelation in the Son not only with the Old Testament but with the whole human quest for God. "No one has ever seen God; the only Son, who is in the bosom of the Father, he has made him known" (v. 18). God is invisible. Nobody has ever seen him, nobody is able to see him. The man who looks at God must die, for God is the Holy One, and we are defiled by sin. Only the begotten Son has seen him. He has made him known. In the Son, the invisible one became visible. "He who has seen me has seen the Father" (John 14:9). In this final clause in v. 18 the absolute and universal claim of the Christian faith is proclaimed.

## The Meaning of Jesus Christ as Logos

Having understood that the prologue is a psalm and having tried to follow its train of thought, we are now in the position to approach our main problem: What is the meaning of the designation of Jesus Christ as "the Word"? Of all the epithets used for Christ in the New Testament, this is the strangest one. We encounter it only in the Johannine writings (John 1:1, 4; 1 John 1:1; Rev 19:13). Several questions arise.

With regard to the origin of this title, I can only make a passing suggestion here. It has often been said, and I myself held the view for a long time, that it originated in Gnosticism. But an examination of the sources has shown, to my surprise, that Wilhelm Bousset was completely right when as many as fifty years ago he observed that the Logos-concept plays a very limited role in Gnosticism.[55] Where it does appear in early Gnosticism—for instance, in the Valentinian School—it is clearly taken from John 1. It is not, therefore, in the field of Gnosticism that we have to seek the prehistory of the Logos-epithet, but in the world of Hellenistic Judaism, where the "Word" was spoken of as the revelation of God. This fact, I believe, has been somewhat obscured in earlier investigations because they started at an unfortunate point. They began with Philo. Philo's Logos concept, however, is but a *potpourri* of Old Testament, Platonic, and Stoic ideas that can hardly be directly connected with the prologue.[56]

But the concept of the personified Logos as a means of God's revelation is much older than Philo. We find it already in the Septuagint. In the powerful description of God's theophany in Habakkuk 3, it says in the Hebrew text that pestilence (*deber*) in unvocalized form is written exactly like "word" (*dabar*).

So it was erroneously translated by *logos* (*dabar*) in the Septuagint, where Habakkuk 3:5 reads: before God "shall come *logos.*" The impact of this concept of the Word as God's precursor is to be seen in Wisdom 18:15-16, where God's Logos is depicted as a stern warrior with a sharp sword leaping down from the royal throne in heaven. This reminds us at once of Revelation 19:11-16, where the coming Christ is described as the hero on the white horse with a sharp sword issuing from his mouth, and where he is called "the Logos of God" (19:13). Thus, perhaps, Christians first used the epithet "the Word of God" as an attribute of the coming Lord. In a second stage the title seems to have been applied to the earthly Lord (1 John 1:1-4) and to the pre-existent Christ (John 1:1-18; 1 John 1:1) as well. If this is correct, the prologue would reflect an advanced stage of the use of the epithet by the church.

But for the present purpose, our attention is focused not upon the problems of origin and development, but rather upon a special and more limited question, namely: What did the epithet "the Logos" mean for the evangelist's contemporaries? This has been strikingly expressed by someone who, at the time when the Gospel of John was written, was probably Bishop of Antioch in Syria. In 110 C.E., about twenty to thirty years after the composition of the Gospel of John, a persecution of the Christians broke out in Antioch. The bishop of the town was arrested and sentenced to be brought to Rome in order to be thrown to the wild beasts in the arena. As he traveled as a prisoner through Asia Minor, the local churches sent messengers to greet him on his way to death. Ignatius, as he was named, in turn sent letters for the churches back with them. These letters are powerful witnesses to the Christian faith. In them, Ignatius encourages the churches to hold fast to their faith and entreats them urgently not to try to free him or to stop him from praising the crucified and risen Lord in the arena, even in the very face of the wild beasts. In the letter to the church of Magnesia, Ignatius speaks of Christ as the Word of God: "Jesus Christ, who is the Word of God, which came forth out of silence" (*Magn.* 8.2).

Ignatius starts with the presupposition that God was silent before he sent Jesus Christ. God's silence is a notion that originated in Judaism, where it was linked with the exegesis of Gen 1:3: "And God said, 'Let there be light.'"[57] What was there before God spoke, asked the rabbis? And their answer was: God's silence (4 Ezra 6:39; *Syr. Bar.* 3:7; Pseudo-Philo, *Bib. Ant.* 60.2).[58] The silence that preceded God's revelation in the creation also preceded the revelation of his wrath against Pharaoh (Wis 18:14), and it will occur again before the new creation (4 Ezra 7:30; *Syr. Bar.* 3:7; Rev 8:1). In the Hellenistic world "Silence" became a symbol of the highest deity. We even have a prayer to Silence. In the Great Magical Papyrus of Paris, the so-called "Mithras Liturgy" (fourth century C.E.), the mystic who, on his way to heaven, is threatened by hostile gods or star-powers is advised to put his finger on his mouth and to ask Silence for help by praying:

> Silence, Silence, Silence—
> symbol of the eternal, immortal God—
> take me under your wings, Silence.[59]

A moving prayer! God is silence. He is utterly removed and does not speak. He is a hidden god. To this inscrutable silence humanity can only lift his hands and cry: "Take me under your wings, Silence."

It is in a world that knew of God's silence as a token of his inexpressible majesty that the message of the Christian Church rings out: God is no longer silent—he speaks. It is true, he has already acted: he revealed his eternal power through the creation, he made known his holy will, he sent his messengers, the prophets. But in spite of all this, he remained full of mystery, incomprehensible, inscrutable, invisible, hidden behind the principalities and powers, behind tribulations and anxieties, behind a mask that was all that could be seen. Still, God has not always remained hidden. There is one point at which God took off the mask; once he spoke distinctly and clearly. This happened in Jesus of Nazareth; this happened, above all, on the cross.

This is how the joyful confession of the psalm in praise of Christ at the beginning of the Gospel of John must have sounded in the ears of those who heard it for the first time: God is no longer silent. God has spoken. Jesus of Nazareth is *the* Word—he is the Word with which God has broken his silence.

## Notes

[1.] *ANET*, 385.

[2.] Jeremias does not attribute this translation.

3. This prayer is called '*Ahabha rabba* and is the second of the benedictions that introduced the *Šema* as prayed every morning and evening. Presumably it was already part of the temple liturgy.

4. There are some isolated occurrences in *Sedher Eliyahu Rabba;* but this is a medieval composition (tenth century?) from southern Italy.

5. Joel Marcus, "A Fifth Ms. of Ben Sira," *JQR* 21 (1930–31) 238.

6. Twenty-one times; sixteen times if parallels are counted only once.

7. Matthew 11:25 / Luke 10:21; Luke 11:2; 22:42; 23:34, 46; John 11:41; 12:27-28; 17:1, 5, 11, 24, 25.

8. Matthew 26:39, 42.

9. Mark 14:36; Matt 11:26 / Luke 10:21; Rom 8:15; Gal 4:6; it appears without the article only in variant readings: John 17:5, 11, 21, 24, 25.

10. It is only in Hasidism (which originated in the eighteenth century) that we find God addressed in familiar ways (for instance, with diminutives), as pointed out to the author by Dr. Jacob Taubes of New York.

11. Karl von Hase, *Die Geschichte Jesu: nach Akademische Vorlesungen*, 2nd ed. (Leipzig: Breitkopf und Härtel, 1876) 422.

12. T. W. Manson, *The Sayings of Jesus* (London: SCM, 1949) 79; Wilfred L. Knox, *Some Hellenistic Elements in Primitive Christianity*, Schweich Lectures 1942 (London: British Academy, 1944) 7.

13. W. D. Davies came to the same conclusion when he compared the role of "knowledge" in Matthew 11:27 and in the Dead Sea Scrolls. He showed that in both cases we find the same combination of eschatological insight and knowledge of God. "'Knowledge' in the Dead Sea Scrolls and Matthew 11:25-30," *HTR* 46 (1953) 113–39; reprinted in *Christian Origins and Judaism* (Philadelphia: Westminster, 1962) 119–42.

14. Gustaf Dalman, *The Words of Jesus*, trans. D. M. Kay (Edinburgh: T. & T. Clark, 1902) 282–83 (German ed. 1898).

[15.] For a view coinciding closely with Jeremias, see C. H. Dodd, *Historical Tradition in the Fourth Gospel* (Cambridge: Cambridge Univ. Press, 1965) 360–61. For a discussion of Jeremias's view and an alternative conclusion, see Ulrich Luz, *Matthew 8–20*, trans. J. E. Crouch, Hermeneia (Minneapolis: Fortress Press, 2001) 164–70. For a redactional and traditio-historical analysis of Matthew 11:25-27, see John Dominic Crossan, *In Fragments: The Aphorisms of Jesus* (San Francisco: Harper and Row, 1983) 191–97.

16. Compare, for example, Mark 4:11; Matthew 11:25; Luke 10:23-24.

17. Irenaeus, *Adv. haer.* 1.13.2; Walter Grundmann, *Die Geschichte Jesu Christi* (Berlin: Evangelische Verlagsanstalt, 1956) 80.

18. For a fuller treatment, see chapter 3.

19. Joachim Jeremias, *The Parables of Jesus*, rev. ed., trans. S. H. Hooke (New York: Scribners, 1972) 190–91.

[20.] For a detailed analysis of Hebrews, see Harold W. Attridge, *Hebrews*, Hermeneia (Philadelphia: Fortress Press, 1989).

21. This may be inferred from the fact that the Eucharist is lacking in Hebrews 6:2, where the subjects of pre-baptismal teaching are enumerated.

[22.] For detailed analyses of 1 Peter, see John H. Elliott, *A Home for the Homeless: A Social-Scientific Criticism of 1 Peter, Its Situation and Strategy*, with a new Introduction (Minneapolis: Fortress Press, 1990); idem, *1 Peter*, AB 37B (New York: Doubleday, 2001); and Paul J. Achtemeier, *1 Peter*, Hermeneia (Minneapolis: Fortress Press, 1996).

23. This was first seen by P. Feine, *Das gesetzesfreie Evangelium des Paulus* (Leipzig: Hinrichs, 1899) 18. The point has been taken up again recently and reinforced by Gert Jeremias, *Der Lehrer der Gerechtigkeit*, SUNT 2 (Göttingen: Vandenhoeck & Ruprecht, 1963) 134–35. [Ed.] For detailed analyses of this

important Galatians passage, see Hans Dieter Betz, *Galatians*, Hermeneia (Philadelphia: Fortress Press, 1979) 148–52; and Philip F. Esler, *Galatians*, NTR (London: Routledge, 1998) 188–91. On the larger topic of this section, see also Ernst Käsemann, "The Saving Significance of the Death of Jesus in Paul," in *Perspectives on Paul*, trans. M. Kohl (Philadelphia: Fortress Press, 1971) 32–59.

[24.] On 1 Corinthians 12:3, see Hans Conzelmann, *1 Corinthians*, Hermeneia (Philadelphia: Fortress Press, 1973); and Richard A. Horsley, *1 Corinthians*, ANTC (Nashville: Abingdon, 1998).

[25.] For the most recent discussion of Isaiah 52:13—53:12, see Klaus Baltzer, *Deutero-Isaiah*, trans. M. Kohl, Hermeneia (Minneapolis: Fortress Press, 2001) 392–429.

26. Detailed evidence (which could be amplified) is available in Walther Zimmerli and Joachim Jeremias, *The Servant of God*, SBT 1/20 (Naperville, Ill.: Allenson, 1957) 88–89, 95–96.

27. Joachim Jeremias, *Heiligengräber in Jesu Umwelt (Mt. 23, 29; Lk. 11, 47): Eine Untersuchung zur Volks-Religion der Zeit Jesu* (Göttingen: Vandenhoeck & Ruprecht, 1958).

28. Zimmerli and Jeremias, *Servant of God*, 103.

29. Joachim Jeremias, *The Eucharistic Words of Jesus*, trans. N. Perrin, rev. ed. (New York: Scribners, 1966; reprint, Philadelphia: Fortress Press, 1977) 131.

30. One finds "many" as a substantive without the article in Isaiah 52:14 and 53:12e. LXX presupposes the word without the article also in 53:11c and 12a.

[31.] For an analysis of the Synoptic relationships and tradition history, see Crossan, *In Fragments*, 285–95.

[32.] For an analysis of Zechariah 13:7-9, see Michael H. Floyd, *Minor Prophets Part 2*, FOTL 22 (Grand Rapids: Eerdmans, 2000) 537–41.

33. It is one of the merits of the late T. W. Manson to have stressed the importance of the esoteric teaching of Jesus in his book, *The Teaching of Jesus: Studies of Its Form and Content*, 2nd ed. (Cambridge: Cambridge Univ. Press, 1948).

[34.] See Gerhard von Rad, *Old Testament Theology*, trans. D. M. G. Stalker (New York: Harper and Row, 1962) vol. 1, 370-95; idem, "Faith Reckoned as Righteousness," in *The Problem of the Hexateuch and Other Essays*, trans. E. W. T. Dicken (New York: McGraw-Hill, 1966) 125-30 (orig. pub. *TLZ* 76 [1951] 129–32); Klaus Koch, "*ṣdq*," in *TLOT* 2.1046–62; and Gottfried Quell and Gottlob Schrenk, "*dikē ktl.*," in *TDNT* 2.174–225.

35. James Hardy Ropes, "Righteousness in the Old Testament and in St. Paul," *JBL* 22 (1903) 211–27.

[36.] The Hebrew term *'ašrē*, rendered by the RSV as "blessed" and the NRSV as "happy," parallels the Greek term *makarios* used in the beatitudes (Matt 5:1-12; Luke 6:20-22). It does not refer, however, to God's blessing or to a positive emotion, but to the value of honor. So these verses are better rendered here with "O how honored are . . ."; see K. C. Hanson, "'How Honorable!' 'How Shameful!' A Cultural Analysis of Matthew's Makarisms and Reproaches," *Semeia* 68 (1996) 81–111.

37. William Wrede, *Paul*, trans. E. Lummis (London: Green, 1907; 2nd German ed. 1908).

38. Albert Schweitzer, *The Mysticism of Paul the Apostle*, trans. W. Montgomery (New York: Holt, 1931; reprint, New York: Macmillan, 1955) 225.

39. Rudolf Schnackenburg, *Baptism in the Thought of St. Paul: A Study in Pauline Theology*, trans. G. R. Beasley-Murray (New York: Herder & Herder, 1964).

40. Rudolf Bultmann, "Das Problem der Ethik bei Paulus," *ZNW* 23 (1924) 123–40.

41. Hans Windisch, "Das Problem des paulinischen Imperativs," *ZNW* 23 (1924) 265–81.

42. Ibid., 278.

43. Rudolf Bultmann, *Theology of the New Testament*, trans. K. Grobel, 2 vols. (New York: Scribners, 1951–55).

44. Martin Luther, *Luther's Works* 37.388.

45. Siegfried Schulz, "Zur Rechtfertigung aus Gnaden in Qumran und bei Paulus," *ZTK* 56 (1959) 155–85; Günter Klein, "Rechtfertigung I," in *RGG*[3] 5.825–28.

46. I have my son, Gert Jeremias, to thank for pointing this out to me. He further referred me to the almost literal parallel to 1QS 11.10-11 that occurs in 1QH 15.12-13, where instead of "justification" (*mišpaṭ*) we read "the inclination of every spirit."

47. See Jeremias, *Parables*, 141–42.

[48.] On ancient Hebrew poetry, see Robert Alter, *The Art of Biblical Poetry* (New York: Basic, 1987); and David L. Petersen and Kent Harold Richards, *Interpreting Hebrew Poetry*, GBS (Minneapolis: Fortress Press, 1992). On hymns from the earliest churches, see Reginald H. Fuller, *The Foundations of New Testament Christology* (New York: Scribners, 1965) 204–27.

49. C. F. Burney, *The Poetry of Our Lord* (Oxford: Clarendon, 1925).

50. Hebrews 1:1-4 is very similar to them but does not show the pattern so distinctively.

51. Hippolytus, *Refutation of All Heresies*, trans. J. H. Macmahon, Ante-Nicene Christian Library 6 (Edinburgh: T. & T. Clark, 1868) 153.

[52.] On gnosticism, see Pheme Perkins, *Gnosticism and the New Testament* (Minneapolis: Fortress Press, 1993); Bentley Layton, *The Gnostic Scriptures: A New Translation with Annotations and Introductions* (New York: Doubleday, 1987); Kurt Rudolph, "Gnosticism," in *ABD* 2.1033–40; and Gregory J. Riley, *Fortress Introduction to Gnosticism* (Minneapolis: Fortress Press, forthcoming).

53. Some scholars combine the last words with those that follow: "What was made, was life in him." But this hardly makes sense. The creation "was" not *zoē*, that is life in the fullest sense. Only the Logos "was" life.

54. It was rather tragic that the commentary on the Gospel of John by Rudolf Bultmann, to which the author is deeply indebted, appeared six years before the Dead Sea Scrolls were found. Bultmann founded his gnostic interpretation of the Fourth Gospel on the assumption that the Johannine dualism is of gnostic origin. But the Scrolls showed that the dualism of the Fourth Gospel has nothing to do with Gnosis but is, rather, Palestinian in origin; for like the dualism of Qumran, it displays three decisive characteristics, each of which is non-gnostic: the Johannine as well as the Essene dualism is monotheistic, ethical, and eschatological (expecting the victory of the light). Rudolf Bultmann, *The Gospel of John*, trans. G. R. Beasley-Murray (Oxford: Blackwell, 1971; German ed. 1941).

55. Wilhelm Bousset, *Kyrios Christos: A History of the Belief in Christ from the Beginning of Christianity to Irenaeus*, trans. J. E. Steely (Nashville: Abingdon, 1970) 386–87; German ed. 1913, p. 305.

[56.] For an example of Philo's Logos-concept, see *Who Is the Heir?* 205–15.

57. Berndt Schaller, *TLZ* 87 (1962) 785.

[58.] For a translation of Palestinian *Targum Neofiti* of Genesis 1:1—2:3 and a discussion of its relevance to John 1:1-18, see Bruce J. Malina and Richard L. Rohrbaugh, *Social-Science Commentary on the Gospel of John* (Minneapolis: Fortress Press, 1998) 35–39.

59. "Mithras Liturgy" lines 558-60, translated from Albrecht Dietrich, *Eine Mithrasliturgie*, 3rd ed. (Darmstadt: Wissenschaftliche Buchgesellschaft, 1966) 6.21. [Ed.] For another English rendering, see Marvin H. Meyer, ed., *The Ancient Mysteries: A Sourcebook* (San Francisco: Harper and Row, 1987) 214.

# Bibliography

## BIBLIOGRAPHY ON THE HISTORICAL JESUS

Allison, Dale C. *Jesus of Nazareth: Millenarian Prophet*. Minneapolis: Fortress Press, 1998.

Borg, Marcus. *Jesus in Contemporary Scholarship*. Valley Forge, Pa. Trinity Press International, 1994.

———. *Meeting Jesus Again for the First Time: The Historical Jesus and the Heart of Contemporary Faith*. San Francisco: HarperSanFrancisco, 1994.

Chilton, Bruce, and Craig A. Evans, eds. *Authenticating the Activities of Jesus*. NTTS 28.2. Leiden: Brill, 1999.

———. *Authenticating the Words of Jesus*. NTTS 28.1. Leiden: Brill, 1999.

———. *Studying the Historical Jesus: Evaluations of the State of Current Research*. NTTS 19. Leiden: Brill, 1994.

Crossan, John Dominic. *The Historical Jesus: The Life of a Mediterranean Jewish Peasant*. San Francisco: HarperSanFrancisco, 1991.

Crossan, John Dominic, and Jonathan L. Reed. *Excavating Jesus: Beneath the Stones, beneath the Texts*. San Francisco: HarperSanFrancisco, 2001.

Duling, Dennis C. *Jesus Christ through History*. New York: Harcourt Brace Jovanovich, 1979.

Herzog, William R. II. *Jesus, Justice, and the Reign of God: A Ministry of Liberation*. Louisville: Westminster John Knox, 2000.

Horsley, Richard A. *Jesus and the Spiral of Violence: Popular Jewish Resistance in Roman Palestine*. Minneapolis: Fortress Press, 1993 [1987].

Horsley, Richard A., and Neil Asher Silberman. *The Message and the Kingdom: How Jesus and Paul Ignited a Revolution and Transformed the Ancient World*. Minneapolis: Fortress Press, 2002 [1997].

Keck, Leander A. *Who Is Jesus? History in the Present Tense*. Studies in the Personalities of the New Testament. Minneapolis: Fortress Press, 2001 [2000].

Malina, Bruce J. *The Social Gospel of Jesus: The Kingdom of God in Mediterranean Perspective*. Minneapolis: Fortress Press, 2001.

Oakman, Douglas E. "The Archaeology of First-Century Galilee and the Social Interpretation of the Historical Jesus." In *SBL 1994 Seminar Papers*, 220–51. Atlanta: Scholars, 1994.

Patterson, Stephen J. *The God of Jesus: The Historical Jesus and the Search for Meaning*. Harrisburg, Pa.: Trinity Press International, 1998.

Reed, Jonathan L. *Archaeology and the Galilean Jesus: A Re-Examination of the Evidence*. Harrisburg, Pa.: Trinity Press International, 2000.

Sanders, E. P. *The Historical Figure of Jesus*. London: Penguin, 1993.

———. *Jesus and Judaism*. Philadelphia: Fortress Press, 1985.

Schweitzer, Albert. *The Quest of the Historical Jesus*. 1st Complete Edition. Edited by John Bowden. Minneapolis: Fortress Press, 2001.

Stegemann, Wolfgang, Bruce J. Malina, and Gerd Theissen, eds. *The Social Setting of Jesus and the Gospels*. Minneapolis: Fortress Press, 2002.

Theissen, Gerd, and Annette Merz. *The Historical Jesus: A Comprehensive Guide*. Translated by John Bowden. Minneapolis: Fortress Press, 1999.

Vermes, Geza. *The Changing Faces of Jesus*. London: Allen Lane, 2000.

———. *Jesus the Jew: A Historian's Reading of the Gospels*. Minneapolis: Fortress Press, 1981.

Wright, N. T. *Jesus and the Victory of God*. Christian Origins and the Question of God 2. Minneapolis: Fortress Press, 1996.

## Bibliography on the Sermon on the Mount

Allison, Dale C. "The Structure of the Sermon on the Mount." *JBL* 106 (1987) 423–45.

Betz, Hans Dieter. *Essays on the Sermon on the Mount*. Translated by L. L. Welborn. Philadelphia: Fortress Press, 1985.

———. *The Sermon on the Mount: A Commentary on the Sermon on the Mount, including the Sermon on the Plain (Matthew 5:3—7:27 and Luke 6:20-49)*. Hermeneia. Minneapolis: Fortress Press, 1995.

———. "The Sermon on the Mount/Plain." In *ABD* 5.1106–12.

Bovon, François. *Luke 1: A Commentary on the Gospel of Luke 1:1—9:50*. Translated by Christine Thomas. Hermeneia. Minneapolis: Fortress Press, 2002.

Carter, Warren. "Some Contemporary Scholarship on the Sermon on the Mount." *Currents in Research: Biblical Studies* 4 (1996) 183–215.

——. *What Are They Saying about Matthew's Sermon on the Mount?* New York: Paulist, 1994.

Davies, W. D. *The Setting of the Sermon on the Mount.* Cambridge: Cambridge Univ. Press, 1966.

Davies, W. D., and Dale C. Allison. *A Critical and Exegetical Commentary on the Gospel according to Saint Matthew.* Vol. 1: *Matthew I–VII.* International Critical Commentary. Edinburgh: T. & T. Clark, 1988.

Guelich, Robert A. *The Sermon on the Mount: A Foundation for Understanding.* Waco: Word, 1982.

Hanson, K. C. "Transformed on the Mountain: Ritual Analysis and the Gospel of Matthew." *Semeia* 67 (1995) 147–70.

Luz, Ulrich. *Matthew 1–7.* Translated by W. C. Linns. Continental Commentaries. Minneapolis: Augsburg, 1989.

——. *The Theology of the Gospel of Matthew.* Translated by Joel Bradford Robinson. New Testament Theology. Cambridge: Cambridge Univ. Press, 1995.

Robinson, James M. "Early Collections of Jesus' Sayings." In *Logia: Les paroles de Jesus. The Sayings of Jesus. Mémorial Joseph Coppens,* edited by J. Delobel et al., 389–94. Bibliotheca ephemeridium theologicarum lovaniensium 59. Leuven: Peeters, 1982.

Schnackenburg, Rudolf. *All Things Are Possible to Believers: Reflections on the Lord's Prayer and the Sermon on the Mount.* Translated by James S. Currie. Louisville: Westminster John Knox, 1995.

Strecker, Georg. *The Sermon on the Mount: An Exegetical Commentary.* Translated by O. C. Dean Jr. Nashville: Abingdon, 1988.

## Bibliography on the Lord's Prayer

Berrigan, Daniel. *The Words Our Savior Gave Us.* Springfield, Ill.: Templegate, 1978.

Betz, Hans Dieter. "Excursus: The Lord's Prayer." In *The Sermon on the Mount: A Commentary on the Sermon on the Mount, including the Sermon on the Plain (Matthew 5:3—7:27 and Luke 6:20-49),* 370–413. Hermeneia. Minneapolis: Fortress Press, 1995.

Boff, Leonardo. *The Lord's Prayer: The Prayer of Integral Liberation.* Translated by T. Morrow. Maryknoll, N.Y.: Orbis, 1983.

Bovon, François. *Luke 1: A Commentary on the Gospel of Luke 1:1—9:50.* Hermeneia. Minneapolis: Fortress Press, 2002.

Gaiser, Frederick J., editor. *The Lord's Prayer,* an issue of *Word and World* 22.1 (winter 2002) [12 articles].

Houlden, J. L. "Lord's Prayer." In *ABD* 4.356–62.

Oakman, Douglas E. "The Lord's Prayer in Social Perspective." In *Authenticating the Words of Jesus*, edited by Bruce Chilton and Craig A. Evans, 137–86. Leiden: Brill, 1999.

Petuchowski, Jakob J., and Michael Brocke, eds. *The Lord's Prayer and Jewish Liturgy*. New York: Seabury, 1978.

Schnackenburg, Rudolf. *All Things Are Possible to Believers: Reflections on the Lord's Prayer and the Sermon on the Mount*. Translated by James S. Currie. Louisville: Westminster John Knox, 1995.

Taussig, Hal. *Jesus before God: The Prayer Life of the Historical Jesus*. Santa Rosa, Calif.: Polebridge, 1999.

Zeller, Deiter, "God as Father in the Proclamation and in the Prayer of Jesus." In *Standing before God: Studies on Prayer in Scriptures and in Tradition with Essays in Honor of John M. Oesterreicher*, edited by Asher Finkel and Lawrence Frizzel, 117–29. New York: Ktav, 1981.

## BIBLIOGRAPHY ON NEW TESTAMENT THEOLOGY

Adam, A. K. M. *Making Sense of New Testament Theology: "Modern" Problems and Prospects*. Studies in American Biblical Hermeneutics 11. Macon, Ga.: Mercer Univ. Press, 1995.

Balla, Peter. *Challenges to New Testament Theology: An Attempt to Justify the Enterprise*. WUNT 2/95. Tübingen: Mohr/Siebeck, 1997.

Brown, Raymond E. *An Introduction to New Testament Christology*. New York: Paulist, 1994.

Caird, G. B. *New Testament Theology*. Edited and completed by L. D. Hurst. Oxford: Clarendon, 1994.

Childs, Brevard S. *The New Testament as Canon: An Introduction*. Philadelphia: Fortress Press, 1984.

Dunn, James D. G. *The Theology of Paul the Apostle*. Grand Rapids: Eerdmans, 1998.

———. *Unity and Diversity in the New Testament: An Inquiry into the Character of Earliest Christianity*. 2nd ed. Philadelphia: Trinity Press International, 1990.

Hultgren, Arland J. *Christ and His Benefits: Christology and Redemption in the New Testament*. Philadelphia: Fortress Press, 1987.

Jeremias, Joachim. *New Testament Theology*. Vol. 1: *The Proclamation of Jesus*. Translated by John Bowden. New York: Scribners, 1971.

Schrage, Wolfgang. *The Ethics of the New Testament*. Translated by David E.

Green. Philadelphia: Fortress Press, 1988.

Strecker, Georg. *Theology of the New Testament.* Translated by M. Eugene Boring. Louisville: Westminster John Knox, 2000.

Stuhlmacher, Peter. *Reconciliation, Law, and Righteousness: Essays in Biblical Theology.* Translated by E. R. Kalin. Philadelphia: Fortress Press, 1986.

Thompson, Marianne Meye. *The Promise of the Father: Jesus and God in the New Testament.* Louisville: Westminster John Knox, 2000.

Via, Dan O. *New Testament Theology.* GBS. Minneapolis: Fortress Press, 2002.

Wright, N. T. *The New Testament and the People of God.* Christian Origins and the Question of God 1. Minneapolis: Fortress Press, 1992.

## WORKS OF JOACHIM JEREMIAS IN ENGLISH

*The Central Message of the New Testament.* New York: Scribners, 1965. Reprint, Philadelphia: Fortress Press, 1981.

*The Eucharistic Words of Jesus.* Translated by Norman Perrin. Rev. ed. New York: Scribners, 1966. Reprint, Philadelphia: Fortress Press, 1977.

*Infant Baptism in the First Four Centuries.* Translated by D. Cairns. Library of History and Doctrine. Philadelphia: Westminster, 1962 (German ed. 1958).

*Jerusalem in the Time of Jesus: An Investigation into Economic and Social Conditions during the New Testament Period.* Translated by F. H. Cave and C. H. Cave. Philadelphia: Fortress Press, 1969 (German ed. 1962; trans. corrected by author up to 1967).

*Jesus' Promise to the Nations.* Translated by S. H. Hooke. SBT 1/24. Naperville, Ill.: Allenson, 1958 (German ed. 1956).

*The Lord's Prayer.* Translated by John Reumann. FBBS 8. Philadelphia: Fortress Press, 1964 (German ed. 1962).

*New Testament Theology.* Vol. 1: *The Proclamation of Jesus.* Translated by John Bowden. New York: Scribners, 1971. [Note: This is the only volume that appeared.]

*The Origins of Infant Baptism: A Further Study in Reply to Kurt Aland.* Translated by Dorothea M. Barton. SHT 1. Naperville, Ill.: Allenson, 1971 (German ed. 1962).

*The Parables of Jesus.* 2nd rev. ed. Translated by S. H. Hooke. New York: Scribners, 1972 (German ed. 1958).

*The Prayers of Jesus.* SBT 2/6. Translated by John Bowden, C. Burchard, and John Reumann. Naperville, Ill.: Allenson, 1967. Reprint, Philadelphia: Fortress Press, 1978 (German ed. 1966).

*The Problem of the Historical Jesus.* Translated by Norman Perrin. FBBS 13. Philadelphia: Fortress Press, 1964 (German ed. 1960).

*Rediscovering the Parables of Jesus.* New York: Scribners, 1966. [Abridged version of *The Parables of Jesus.*]

*The Sermon on the Mount.* Translated by Norman Perrin. FBBS 2. Philadelphia: Fortress Press, 1963 (German ed. 1959).

(With Walther Zimmerli). *The Servant of God.* SBT 1/20. Naperville, Ill.: Allenson, 1957 (German ed. 1952).

*The Rediscovery of Bethesda, John 5:2.* NTAM 1. Louisville: Southern Baptist Theological Seminary, 1966 (German ed. 1949).

*Unknown Sayings of Jesus.* Translated by Reginald H. Fuller. Rev. ed. London: SPCK, 1964 (German ed. 1949).

## FESTSCHRIFTEN IN HONOR OF JOACHIM JEREMIAS

Lohse, Eduard, et al., eds. *Der Ruf Jesu und die Antwort der Gemeinde. Exeget. Untersuchungen. Joachim Jeremias z. 70. Geburtstag gewidmet von seinen Schülern.* Göttingen: Vandenhoeck & Ruprecht, 1970.

Stauffer, Ethelbert, editor. *Judentum, Urchristentum, Kirche: Festschrift für Joachim Jeremias.* BZNW 26. Berlin: Töpelmann, 1960.

# Index of Authors

*Editor's Note: Dates have been supplied for authors of earlier generations in order to provide historical context.*

## MODERN AUTHORS

## ANCIENT AND MEDIEVAL AUTHORS

# Index of Terms and Phrases

# Index of Ancient Sources

FORTRESS CLASSICS *in* BIBLICAL STUDIES